Esien Emana Akpan The African Problems

Esien Emana Akpan The African Problems

KING SOLOMON SPIRITUAL LIBRARY
THE GOD ENCYCLOPAEDIA WORD OF INFINITY

BY
THE SPIRIT OF THE FATHER GOD
THROUGH HIS SERVANT
**HRM KING SOLOMON DAVID
JESSE ETE**
(King Solomon Spiritual Library)
Eteroyal Universal Family - BCS

All rights reserved
Copyright © Solomon ETE, 2008
Solomon ETE is hereby identified as author of this work in accordance with Section 77 of the Copyright, Designs and Patents Act 1988

The book cover picture is copyright to Solomon ETE

This book is published by
King Solomon Spiritual Library
P O BOX 27394
London E12 6WW UK
www.ksslibrary.com
www.kingsolomonspirituallibrary.com

This book is sold subject to the conditions that it shall not, by way of trade or otherwise, be lent, resold, hired out or otherwise circulated without the author's or publisher's prior consent in any form of binding or cover other than that in which it is published and without a similar condition including this condition being imposed on the subsequent purchaser.

A CIP record for this book is available from the British Library

ISBN 97-0-9559801-4-5

ESIEN EMANA AKPAN THE AFRICAN PROBLEMS
=====
THE SECRET OF THE UNIVERSAL PROBLEM AND THE REMEDY

Contents

Chapter One   **15-75**

BEYOND THE HUMAN KNOW

Introduction:

A: What Is This Again

B: This Is Information Of The Father God Almighty

C: Not All The People Will Understand And Believe This Information

D: I THE FATHER GOD The Supreme Word The Creator Of Heaven And Earth

E: The Word Of The Father's Talk God Present Is Beyond What The

Human Know

F: The Father's Talk Is Not Your History Of The World By Humans

G: I The Father God The Creator Of The Universe Bring Some Of My Records That Were Before Anything Existed

Conclusion A: In Case You Do Not Understand Some Parts Of The Father's Talk God Present

Conclusion B: Come And Go

Conclusion C: I Am Where, Here And There

Chapter Two   **77-248**

ESIEN EMANA AKPAN

Part One: **INTRODUCTION**

A: The First Of Everything

B: Low Mentality Is Lack Of Love For One Another

C: The Result Of Lack Of Love

D: The First Root Of Evil

E: Spiritual Civilization Came From Improvement Of Love

F: Are You Still In Yesterday's Spirit Of Elementary Self?

G: You Must Conquer The Evil Spirit Of Elementary Self.

Chapter Two   *127-248*

Part Two: **AKPAN**

Introduction

A: Akpan Means The Spirit Nature

B: Akpan Means The First Formula Of Everything

C: What Happens If You Take That Same Nature Of Akpan

D: The Akpan Problem Is Natural

E: The First Thought Cannot Be Perfect

F: Do Not Pray To Be The First Or The Last

G: Akpan Is The First And Also The Last

Chapter Two   166-248
Part Three: **AFRICAN PROBLEMS**

Introduction: Esien Emana Akpan

A: First Thing Is Alone And Empty

B: Esien Emana Akpan

C: How To Solve Akpan The African Problem

D: The Power Of Akpan Is By His Word

E: Check Well All Akpan And All First Positions Or First Ideas
What Happened Check Well

F: Even Though Everything Is In The Position Of Akpan

G: My New Order And The Only Tradition Akpan Must Follow Is Love Unity And Peace

Chapter Two   211-248
Part Four: **CONCLUSIONS**

Introduction: The Remedy

A: Second Thought Is The Remedy For All Akpan Problems

B: This Is He End Problems For African Nations

C: You Must Be Subjected To The Truth Life Of The Father God

D: You Must Not Worship Any Idol

E: You Must Humble Yourself In Your Father's House Africans

F: Akpan The Firstborn In The World Should Love

G: Akpan Must Join In The Celebration Of The Universal Supreme Word Season Celebration

H: All Akpan To Take Evolution From Negative Nature Of Cain Lucifer Representative On Earth

I: Then I The Supreme Word Of The Universe Will Do What

Ao: The Lecture Revelation Is The Remedy For All Problems In Africa, Akpan And Everybody In The Whole Universe

Chapter Three   *249-288*
"A" OF A TO Z

Chapter Four   *289-400*
THE UNIVERSAL PROBLEM AND THE REMEDY

Part One: **The Problem Of Mankind**

Introduction: The Launching Of The Great Universal Change

A: Adam And Eve

B: I The Father God Speaks The Word

C: Cain And Abel

D: Abraham And His Two Sons

E: Ishmael And Isaac

F: Isaac And His Two Sons

G: Esau And Jacob

Chapter Four   **329-400**
Part Two: **PRESENT ACTION PLAN**

Introduction: The Birth And Death Of Our Lord Jesus Christ The Universal Spiritual God The Father

A: My Plan Was To End The Problem Through The Birth Of Christ

B: Who Was The Barrier To The Program

C: My Plan Was To End The Problem Through Esau And Jacob

D: The Second Barrier

E: **My Next Plan Was To End The Problem Through Jacob And Joseph**

F: The Third Barrier

G: The Final Action Plan The Birth And The Death Of Christ

Chapter Four   **359-400**
Part Three: **THE CONCLUSION THE REMEDY**

Introduction:
This Is Your Last And Final Chance

A: I Have Finally Come Out To Speak Openly To All Humankind

B: The Problem Of The First Nature Is Now Over Through The Lecture

Revelation Of Esien Emana Akpan Titled, Akpan The African Problem

C: All Nations Of The World Are One

D: One Spirit One Love One Life And One Father And Mother Of All Things Brotherhood

E: **I** Mean Business Now!

F: Enough Is Enough

G: Esien Emana Akpan Ended With The Father God Almighty

H: No More Negative Self Glory

I: Only The Positive Of Myself Shall Be Glorified From Now

Ao: There Is Peace Everywhere Here And There In The Entire Universe

Chapter Five   **401-445**
THE INSPIRATIONAL WRITERS

Chapter One

BEYOND HUMAN KNOW PURELY SPIRITUAL

FATHER'S TALK
(GOD PRESENT)

Date: Noah Ninth Alpheus, **Father** Two Thousand And Eight (OI.AB.BOOH)
Tuesday Ninth December Year Two Thousand And Eight (09.12.2008)

In the Name of Our Lord Jesus Christ, In the Blood of Our Lord Jesus Christ, Now and forever more

Today! It PLEASES **ME THE FATHER GOD THE CREATOR OF THE UNIVERSE, THE SUPREME UNIVERSAL WORD THE CREATOR OF HEAVEN AND EARTH** to give this short Lecture Revelation titled: **BEYOND HUMAN KNOW PURELY SPIRITUAL**

INTRODUCTION

As **I** always say, let every human heart be clean and clear and be with humility and understanding with LOVE to hear from **THE FATHER GOD** once again. If you have this faith and that belief then, the communication between you and **I** will flow very well. However, if you withhold your heart from **ME THE FATHER GOD** by hiding yourself and having a double mind due to doubts and not believing in **ME**, then the communication of understanding will be influenced by your thoughts as you do not believe **THE FATHER GOD**. That is the reason **I** bring all manners of information and explanations about **THE FATHER'S TALK (GOD PRESENT)**.

I want you to believe that **THE FATHER'S TALK (GOD PRESENT)** information is NOT motivated by cunning or by the human mind. It is NOT the WORD from a studio of carnality. It is NOT a broadcast by evil or by the second thought of a human being. **THE FATHER'S TALK (GOD PRESENT)** information is a direct broadcast, straight from **THE FATHER GOD**. They are broadcasted directly from the studio of **THE FATHER GOD ALMIGHTY THE SUPREME WORD OF THE UNIVERSE.**

All **THE FATHER'S TALK (GOD PRESENT)** Lecture Revelations are direct from **THE FATHER GOD ALMIGHTY THE CREATOR OF THE UNIVERSE,** why **THE FATHER'S TALK (GOD PRESENT)** always mention as Lecture Revelation is because you do not need anyone to interpret any **WORD** of **THE FATHER'S TALK (GOD PRESENT)** to you. That is why **I** call this WISDOM, '**BEYOND THE HUMAN KNOW**'.

When **I EXIST, I WAS, WAS, WAS**, this information was in existence with **ME** and that means that indirectly, **I THE FATHER GOD**

ALMIGHTY THE SUPREME WORD OF THE UNIVERSE, AM revealing **MYSELF** to humankind once again. I do this so that you would not continue to think that **I THE FATHER GOD** does not speak directly with human beings anymore. And most importantly, this **FATHER'S TALK** (**GOD PRESENT**) Lecture Revelations are NOT via any angel. They are not inspirational outcomes from one possessed by an angel or a ghost. They are directly from *"THE SUPREME SILENT THOUGHT OF CREATION"*, **THE FATHER GOD'S** 'POSSESSING HEART' **THE UNIVERSAL SUPREME WORD**. I TAKE OVER THE BODY, THE SOUL AND SPIRIT OF His Royal Majesty KING SOLOMON DAVID JESSE **ETE** the incarnated King Solomon David of Israel who was also incarnate ABEL the second positive son of Adam THAT **I** NOW TALK THROUGH.

This particular Lecture Revelation that points out that this is **Beyond**

What Human Know serves as a preface to all **THE FATHER'S TALK (GOD PRESENT)** Lecture Revelations. This information should come before the main Lecture Revelation. You know that you are not reading the words of the chairman of your local council or the words of the leader of your church or the words of a president or a prime minister or the words of any human being. This information is called **THE FATHER'S TALK (GOD PRESENT)** because it comes directly from **ME THE FATHER GOD THE CREATOR OF THE UNIVERSE**.

THE FATHER GOD ALMIGHTY is the **SPIRIT** that motivated **THE WORD**, that created **THE WORD** and made **THE WORD** come to be in existence and this is the **SPIRIT** that is talking now as **THE FATHER'S TALK (GOD PRESENT)**.

The reason **I AM** bringing this particular short **FATHER'S TALK (GOD PRESENT)** Lecture Revelation, is so that when you read, **THE FATHER'S TALK (GOD PRESENT)** Lecture Revelations or listen to any of them by accessing them in anyway, do not attribute them to ordinary vision or prophesy. This is not a discussion but a Revelation Information from the **Archive Record**, THE KING SOLOMON SPIRITUAL LIBRARY- **The Boom Heart of THE FATHER GOD** where all the information is kept. It is only when and how **I** want the information to come that the information will come.

It is not a case of starting to think about what to say and what to write or doing a research. Therefore, when you read or listen to any of **THE FATHER'S TALK (GOD PRESENT)** Lecture Revelations and you don't believe, then at the end of the day, you have yourself to blame.

A: **WHAT IS THIS AGAIN**

When **I** searched in the Spiritual Supreme Memory of **MYSELF**, which is where all hearts of human beings came from by creation, the percentage of seventy-five percent ask this question in spirit: **What Is This Again**? In other words they are asking where the information came from. Who brings them out? That is why **I AM** bringing out this particular information to answer the question. It means that most of all hearts that is, seventy-five percent of all the hearts are asking **THE FATHER GOD, What Is This Again**.

This **FATHER'S TALK (GOD PRESENT)** Lecture Revelation title is *AFTER THOSE DAYS SAYS THE LORD MOST HIGH* prophesied by Isaiah.

AFTER THOSE DAYS SAYS THE LORD MOST HIGH is THE TESTIMONY OF EVERLASTING **WORD, EVERLASTING SUPREME WORD OF THE FATHER GOD**, AND THE

TESTIMONY OF **THE HOLY SPIRIT OF TRUTH** PERSONIFIED ON EARTH.

When **I** attended to this job physically and finished it, **I** had to keep the record of **MY** WORK and the record could not come direct from **MY** human person personified. It had to come from The **Servant** as the **Witness**. And that Servant and the Witness must be motivated and interacted together with **ME** so that whatever He would say will not come from the human mind but will come from the heart of **THE FATHER GOD**. This **Servant** and **Witness** is His Royal Majesty (HRM) King Solomon David Jesse **ETE**. He is **MY Servant** and **Witness** that **I AM** directly involved with from the time of The Beginning when **I LIVED BEYOND THE HUMAN KNOW**.

BEYOND THE HUMAN KNOW is before creations.

BEYOND THE HUMAN KNOW is before even the SOUND that manifested THE SPOKEN WORD, a formulation by **ME THE FATHER GOD** in the '*hidinan'* – the centre where the sound formed '**GEN**' OF LIFE in the middle of the A***kwavor.***

Akwavor is where **I** generated **MYSELF** on top of the water. You will see most of this information in other **FATHER'S TALK (GOD PRESENT)** Lecture Revelation.

Where **I** generated **MYSELF** and formed the steam of **MY** energy on top of the water is called *akwavor.* And **MY** energy brought out the sound and then the water from the steam rushed back to the **deep** called ***Odu Idem Abasi***. When the water was rushing back to ***Odu Idem Abasi***, the rushing force generated the sound and the energy of the sound produced the **Gen** of **THE SPOKEN WORD "THE CREATOR"**. And this place called ***Odu Idem Abasi*** (THE HARDWARE OF THE SPIRIT) is where the rushing force of energy of creation comes from and goes back before the sun breaks out the following day. That is why **I AM** telling you that this information titled **BEYOND THE HUMAN KNOW** therefore **THE FATHER'S TALK (GOD PRESENT)** information is beyond the sphere of human beings. That is, the information that existed before the existence of creation.

There was nothing like human beings and there was nothing like souls. But there was something as something called **SOMETHING, THE SUPREME THOUGHT (THE DIVINE LOVE THE UNIVERSAL SUPREME WORD)** that eventually came to be born as Our Lord Jesus Christ. That is the potency **I** used to create Adam and lived in Adam, as **I THE FATHER'S TALK (GOD PRESENT)**. When **I** say **THE FATHER'S TALK (GOD PRESENT)**, **I** mean **I, -THIS SUPREME WORD**. So, that is the answer to the question that seventy-five percent of the human souls ask as '**What Is This Again**?'

This is EVERLASTING TESTIMONY ABOUT THE **SUPREME WORD OF THE UNIVERSE, THE PERSONIFIED HOLY SPIRIT OF TRUTH**. This is the last information that humankind will live with by from **THE FATHER GOD AND IS LIVED BY THE FATHER GOD**. From **THE FATHER GOD** live by **THE FATHER GOD** and with **THE FATHER GOD ALMIGHTY**. Then everything will be **THE FATHER GOD! THE FATHER GOD! THE FATHER GOD! FATHER! FATHER! FATHER GOD ALMIGHTY**! Call no one FATHER except **THE SUPREME FATHER**. Of all the human beings on earth, it is one person that is **THE FATHER**. Also of the humans on earth it is only one person that is **the Servant**. These are the representative of the **THOUGHT** and the **WORD**. The body where those two things live called Adam is **THE KING OF KINGS AND THE LORD OF LORDS**. So, you have one **FATHER** and one **LORD** and that is **THE KING OF KINGS** and **THE LORD OF LORDS**. Every other person is a servant of **THE FATHER GOD** that is, sons and daughters of **THE FATHER GOD**. Therefore, with this Revelation you don't need to ask, **'What Is This Again'**.

You know, yesterday, today and tomorrow **I AM** the same and because of that, you will NEVER know the way of **THE FATHER GOD** because the more you look the less you see.

B: **THIS IS INFORMATION OF THE FATHER GOD ALMIGHTY**

This is not information of your father, your brother, your sister, your mother, your husband, your wife, your president, your King, your Queen or yourself. It is not! **THIS IS INFORMATION FROM THE FATHER GOD ALMIGHTY, THE CREATOR OF THE UNIVERSE**. It is NOT from angel. So, when you are reading or listening to the information clarify your heart.

In fact, **I** have said this time without number that the number of people and the human beings that will show respect whenever they come across **THE FATHER'S TALK (GOD PRESENT)** Lecture Revelations will be so many. The **GOD PRESENT, I** put in **THE FATHER'S TALK** is to show you that **I MYSELF THE SUPREME WORD OF THE UNIVERSE, AM THE FATHER'S TALK (GOD PRESENT)** Lecture Revelations. If you believe the contents of any piece of publication that carries **THE FATHER'S TALK (GOD PRESENT)** Lecture Revelations that testifies about **THE EVERLASTING GOSPEL, THE EVERLASTING WORDS OF GOD, THE SUPREME WORD OF THE FATHER GOD** that has come to reconstruct the world, then you are blessed. By believing this testimony you are okay and **I** mean totally okay! Even, if you die, **I** can return you to the earth immediately to witness this **WORD. I** can do anything at all.

When you talk about miracles happening again then you should know that this is the only miracle that can happen. There is no miracle again to occur. The **TOTAL POTENCY** of **THE FATHER GOD** is behind **THE FATHER'S TALK (GOD PRESENT)** Lecture Revelations.

THE FATHER'S TALK (GOD PRESENT) information is to replace all negative information and energy on earth. **THE FATHER'S TALK (GOD PRESENT)** information has come to stay in three capacities in the **spirit**, the **soul** and the **physical**. THIS IS **THE SUPREME WORD OF THE UNIVERSE**.

C: **NOT ALL THE PEOPLE WILL UNDERSTAND AND BELIEVE THIS INFORMATION**

I know 'you' if you don't believe and **I** know 'you' if you believe this information. It is not every human soul that will believe, because it is in the record that one quarter of the human race are the positive ones and are the ones that will believe.

That is, if you divide the entire humanity into four parts, it is only one part out of the whole four parts that are positive human beings and these are the ones that will believe **THE FATHER'S TALK (GOD PRESENT)** information. The remaining three quarters of human beings will start misbehaving. That is why the real humans, the Human-Gods, the positive human beings from Adam and Eve, the stock of Abel, are the Servants of Christ as the Servants of THE KING OF KINGS. They are all Kings and Queens, Princes and Princesses. They are the houses of **THE SUPREME WORD**.

The doubting human beings prove themselves to be negative. They are not supposed to doubt if they are all Human-Gods. Animals, birds and fish that took evolution and become sub-human beings are the doubters because they are struggling to pas exams. But for the Human-Gods, **I THE FATHER GOD** in them passed the exams for them. That is, if you believe **THE FATHER GOD**, you practice LOVE ONE ANOTHER then, you are with **THE FATHER GOD**. That is why it is said that not all children of Abraham are real children of Abraham. Some are not real children of Abraham. The evolutional human beings as those from animals, birds and fish are not the real children of Abraham. But the real human beings as the house of everything, the Centre of Development represent **THE FATHER GOD** and that is why any human beings can be doubtful of this.

When you see somebody that has no love that practices evil, that has hatred for one another, that gossips, and practices negativism of any form, and is not peaceful and does not treat people well, that is are the sorts of persons that can doubt. Maybe the creation of that person is more animal than human-God due to transfusion of blood through fornication and adultery.

Other than that the real Human-God that is born and activated by **ME THE FATHER GOD** cannot be hardhearted. Even if the person is annoyed, very annoyed, after a while the annoyance will evaporate.

Even if you are annoyed as a positive child of **THE FATHER GOD** your annoyance should not exceed twelve hours.

You cannot harbour evil.
You cannot kill.
You cannot do anything evil.

The positive children of **THE FATHER GOD** can however be annoyed by instinct if somebody offends them, but immediately they will correct themselves. These are the telltale signs of the different characteristics that the positive and negative people portray. So, if you come across yourself to be negative in any form, pray very hard. If your conscience is blaming you, pray very hard and take evolution away from that negativism. If not one day, one hour, one minute, one second and in one week, one month, one year and with time, all evil on earth shall confess and they shall cease to function as **I** switch off the light in **MY** back. That will be the melting point and end of all negativism. If that great day meets you, if the **Total Great Change** meets you and you have not changed for good then ***THE GREAT UNIVERSAL CHANGE*** will overtake you and you are finished! It is not going to be one day as people think. It can happen to individuals at different times that is, within the periods of time **I** have mentioned. It can happen to you in a second, in a minute or in an hour. The great change can come to you any day. And if that faithful day of reckoning arrives you will be at your wits end. So, you have to change now when **THE GREAT CHANGE** has not reached you. Change voluntarily to the positive side of **THE FATHER GOD**. If you believe this, it will be the beginning of your change to positivism.

Naturally it is not all the people on earth that will believe this information. However, if anybody attempts to make any comment in this regard, tell the person to read at least seven **FATHER'S TALK (GOD PRESENT)** Lecture Revelations before making any comments about the information of **THE FATHER'S TALK (GOD PRESENT)**. If the person does not listen to you and still makes a bad comment, leave the person for **THE FATHER GOD ALMIGHTY**. Don't do anything harmful or unpleasant to the person. Just leave the person with his or her ways. It just shows that such a person is a human-animal, human-bird or human-fish.

D: I THE FATHER GOD THE SUPREME WORD THE CREATOR OF HEAVEN AND EARTH

I AM THE ONE that is giving this Lecture Revelation to go before every of **THE FATHER'S TALK (GOD PRESENT)** Lecture Revelations. This is so that when you go in to read the main Lecture Revelation or listen to it, you would have prepared your mind and come to the decision that you are not dealing with human words, but words from **THE FATHER GOD ALMIGHTY**. The Lecture Revelations are Spiritual history of events.

You sometimes read books for academic purposes. Some of the books you buy and read are written by professors, PhD holders, Master degree holders and also people with no such qualifications, the ordinary people, including a dreamer and also a prophet. Just about anybody can write a book. However, the information of **THE FATHER'S TALK**

(**GOD PRESENT**) Lecture Revelations, come direct from **THE FATHER GOD'S** Library, THE COMPREHENSIVE AND ABILITY MEMORY OF GOD, thus, the information there is different and they are LECTURE REVELATIONS where **I** speak in a plain language.

If you are positive and while going through any of the Lecture Revelations of **THE FATHER'S TALK (GOD PRESENT)** and you get confused about something, you can write, but with a good spirit, to HRM King Solomon David Jesse **ETE** or email Him to get a response. There is no problem about that.

Everyone should nevertheless be aware that asking questions for clarification is open only to those who want to develop as Higherself students to know **THE FATHER GOD** more. That is why **I** ask HRM King Solomon David **ETE** to establish a school called **The School of The Higherself Brotherhood Mastership** so that if you want to know more or you have questions you can direct your questions there. Do not ask **ME THE FATHER GOD** that is, in a carnal way. Don't ask **ME** any question you know to be negative. But if you ask **ME** a question in which you want to know more, then **I, THE FATHER GOD** will even answer you before your question reaches HRM King Solomon **ETE** because **I** live in every heart. If anyone activates **ME** in their heart and humble himself or herself then **I THE FATHER GOD** will reveal **MYSELF** to you.

E: **THE WORD OF THE FATHER'S TALK (GOD PRESENT) IS BEYOND WHAT ANY HUMAN BEING KNOW**

I speak as **I** know and you think, as you know. What you don't know is what you don't know. What **I** know is what **I** know. So, this information is beyond what you know. What is it that humanity knows? Is it the History of the world? What do you know about the history of the world? It is only **I, THE FATHER GOD** that can give the history of the world.

People have done all sorts of things and formulated all sorts of stories about the world. Because they thought, where is **THE FATHER GOD** to speak for **HIMSELF**? Human beings compare the information contained in **THE FATHER'S TALK (GOD PRESENT)** with their research. Where did you research and get your information from? Where did you get the records of these periods for your research five hundred years and one thousand years ago?

Some people say **THE FATHER GOD** wrote in Arabic. Some claim **THE FATHER GOD** spoke in Hebrew, Aramaic, French or English or this language or that language. None of that is the language of **THE FATHER GOD**.

MY language is the SPIRIT and **MY** language is THE SPOKEN WORD. And **MY** School Centre is the **THOUGHT** and **MY** Workshop, the Word and **MY**

Supreme Premises is this world. So, you cannot give account of **ME THE FATHER GOD** but **I** can give account of everything.

I can enter you to bring out information that was before creation and that nobody knew about. Therefore, since THE SPIRIT lives, lives, lives and lives right from the beginning of time without beginning and without ending, conclusively it is THE SPIRIT alone has all the RECORDS and can bring them out any time.

That is why you have prophecies.

That is why you have inspirations.

That is why you have visions and dreams.

That is also why you have this one called **possessing spirit** that takes over the person completely and use for its own purpose. Those who practice some kind of invocations and some kind of manipulations in a negative way know what **I AM** talking about.

If a witch can enter into somebody to act, if mammy water that is, spirit-souls in the water can come out physically and take an assumed body of people and inspire them to talk; if your papa and mama that died as ghost can enter into somebody and talk, how else do you expect **I THE FATHER GOD ALMIGHTY, THE CREATOR OF THE UNIVERSE, THE SUPREME SPIRIT OF ALL THINGS** to communicate. You think **I** cannot talk, is it not so?

Human beings really think **I** cannot talk. Where do you get all the manipulations you do? Everything that you indulge in called spiritual work, invocation, magic, juju and this and that are all second hand spirit-souls that are you using.

When **I** use something for positive purposes and pass them out as waste, they become second hand spirits souls. Since these spirit-souls have nothing to eat they try what is known as imitation. They use imitation actions to attend to your invocations. All that negative things they do for you are so that they can eat. So don't think you possess any truthful information apart from that of **THE FATHER GOD**.

All the information that **I THE FATHER GOD** inspired people in a positive way to provide is called **FATHER'S TALK**. But they were not revealed in this manner. They called them the Word of God. And you know that every good spirit-soul means God and even every human being is a God. Spirit means SPIRIT GOD. But the name God came out from good that is, THE GOOD SELF OF **THE FATHER GOD**.

All the negative things called evil, Satan, demon, devil is all the same, and something you cannot see with your naked eyes. All the good things you cannot see with your naked eyes are GODS from **THE FATHER GOD**. And all the things you cannot see which are negative are Satan, evil, demon, and devil. They are elementary self, from **Second Hand Spirits souls**. So those negative spirits souls are second hand thoughts. It is like when you finish speaking and somebody copies your speech and goes and speaks them wrongly, gossiping and imitating in such instances.

Therefore, all positive ideas, positive words, positive arrangements, positive preaching or sermons and all the positive words of God are from **THE FATHER GOD** and they are also **THE FATHER'S TALK**, but not **GOD PRESENT**. They are **FATHER'S TALK** because I inspired them.

If you talk with **love** it is **THE FATHER'S TALK**.

If you talk with **peace** it is **THE FATHER'S TALK**.

If you give good advice it is **THE FATHER'S TALK**.

If you say good morning with a clean heart, it is **THE FATHER'S TALK**. If you say **peace** to someone it is **THE FATHER'S TALK**. Any positive pronouncement is **THE FATHER'S TALK** because **THE FATHER GOD** is the Spirit that motivates you to be alive. So, you are not even the one that is talking.

Suppose all Presidents of all the countries of the world, All Prime Ministers, Senators, all ministers, all State Governors, all chairmen of local authorities, all church leaders, all human beings including the small men, big men, small women, big women speak positively from **THE FATHER GOD,** then everything will be well on this earth. But since you speak negative and think negative that is why you give room to Satan to talk through you. That is why you give room to all the things that do not bring glory to **THE FATHER GOD**. Nonetheless, now is the end of all those negativisms, since **THE FATHER'S TALK (GOD PRESENT)** has arrived.

It would not matter the number of people that will be annoyed for **THIS FATHER'S TALK (GOD PRESENT)** INFORMATION. It does not matter how many people that will not be happy about **THE FATHER'S TALK (GOD PRESENT)** Lecture Revelations. What really matters is that **I AM TALKING** and **I** WILL BE TALKING FOR ETERNITY. For **ME** to release SEVENTY-TWO MILLION titles of LECTURES REVELATIONS for KING SOLOMON SPIRITUAL LIBRARY, should alert you to the fact that this is not a joke. **I** mean Seventy-two million titles of **THE FATHER'S TALK (GOD PRESENT)** Lecture Revelations and that represents **Seventy-two Million Positive Selves of THE FATHER GOD**, in diverse forms. So, **I** cover seventy-two hours that is, three days and three nights energy of creation. That also covers Seven Spirits of Creations of **THE FATHER GOD** of which the Head of them is called **THE KING OF KINGS AND THE LORD OF LORDS** who is **The**

Father Of All Human-Gods. Therefore, if you like you believe, if you like don't believe. But you cannot do anything about it because the **WORD** that created you and lives in you will control your mind and **HE IS THE FATHER GOD ALMIGHTY THE SUPREME WORD OF THE UNIVERSE.**

F: **THE FATHER'S TALK IS NOT YOUR HISTORY OF THE WORLD BY HUMANS**

As **I** said earlier **THE FATHER'S TALK (GOD PRESENT)** INFORMATION is not the history from your historian. It is not the work of archaeology where you dig and dig the ground for the corpse of the dead. A corpse that cannot stay up to one hundred years when put in the ground is what you are digging? Anything that is dead that you decide to pick physically in this world to gather information from could not have stayed up to one thousand years from the day of burial. But now that **I** have the digital world in physical existence you will see many things because information can now stay more than one million years and forever, because we are now in the digital world. Previously, things that were preserved eventually faded away, because even if you carve the thing in stone the information eventually erodes when it is rubbed by air.

So many things go into extinction. So many things as even iron and stone can cease to be, but the Spirit can never go into extinction. That is why digital products have come to make photographs stay for long and information can stay for long because you would not see it, but it exist. That is what **I, THE FATHER GOD ALMIGHTY** have done.

I have come in several different ways to put many things in place. However, some of these human beings **I** use for all the inventions and innovations think they are the ones that did them. But it does not matter because the fact remains that **I AM** the ACTIVATOR in every heart and everything.

I AM the **ONE** that does everything, but the negative mind turned those things to be negative. If you do anything negative, you will pay for being negative. But if you do anything positive, you will be blessed for being positive. Therefore, the meaning of **THE FATHER GOD** is **THE ACTIVATOR OF LIFE**. **HE** is the life in every soul. That is the reason that the CAPITAL ADVICE of **THE FATHER'S TALK (GOD PRESENT)** is **Love One Another** and

Thou shalt not hate anybody.

Thou shalt not kill or plan to kill anybody not even yourself. And

Thou Shalt Not Hurt Anybody.

Those are the CAPITAL ADVICE. Leave everybody alone! What you should do is to help one another to live, to be alive and to be happy. That is the duty **I** give to all human beings.

Therefore, the information of **THE FATHER'S TALK (GOD PRESENT)** is not your world history, so, do not go and compare this with your history. THIS IS BEYOND THE HISTORY OF THE PHYSICAL UNIVERSE. These are digital information's that **I** have brought back on earth. At the same time when you come across information of **THE FATHER'S TALK (GOD PRESENT)** that is controversial to your history, take whichever one you like to take.

If you want to believe the information from **THE FATHER GOD** you can. If it is the information provided by the historians of the world you choose to believe over **MINE**, you can do so, but remember that the information they gave is based on research from another human source. And sometimes when they are hungry they tell fibs of reaching where they never actually went.

For instance, somebody says that they went to Israel and toured the whole land of Israel. Maybe the person only went to Jerusalem, Capernaum and few other places and came back. Whom did this person ask questions about Israel? You do not know there for all the things that they present only about thirty-five percent will be correct. The rest are false because they reckon that they must keep something for stories that they have all the records. Nonetheless, the actual inspiration for the Holy Bible is true. The words of Bible are inspirations of **THE FATHER GOD** and not eyewitness account per se. Therefore, what you should believe is **THE WORD**, which **THE FATHER GOD** can inspire and enter into someone and force the person to speak and give the record and information of something nobody knew and even the person giving that record at the time never knew. That is what **I** want you to know. **I** want you to know the difference between **THE FATHER'S TALK (GOD PRESENT)** information and other talks. Some of the information **I** will bring out will marvel you and you will think twice about what is going on. THIS IS **BEYOND THE KNOWN, BEYOND YOUR IMAGINATION, BEYOND** and **WHAT HUMAN KNOWS**.

G: **I THE FATHER GOD THE CREATOR OF THE UNIVERSE BRING SOME OF MY RECORDS THAT WERE BEFORE ANYTHING EXISTED**

This is the information of before anything existed physically. This is the film of nature. What **I** have in **THOUGHT** are what **I AM** bringing out now.

I AM bringing out this information now because the final, final verdict of all things will come.

THE REASON **I DEFER THE FINAL JUDGMENT** AND WHY ***THE GREAT UNIVERSAL CHANGE*** IS STILL WAITING FOR PEOPLE IS BECAUSE YOU NEED TO HEAR THIS INFORMATION.

That is why **I** will really, really bless any soul, any human being that helps in whatsoever way to put this information of **THE FATHER'S TALK (GOD PRESENT)** across to as many people as you can, even to the entire humanity. You are blessed from the very time you accept to do that! And also, **I THE SUPREME WORD** and, **THE SUPREME INFORMATION** will register **MYSELF** in a positive way in you.

You will see that your environment will change for good when you are happy about this **WORD** and you decide to promote, help to circulate and to work in any manner to spread the INFORMATION OF **THE FATHER'S TALK (GOD PRESENT), THE EVERLASTING TESTIMONY OF THE**

FATHER GOD to enlighten the whole world. **MY OWN** time to act is according to how many people hear this information. **I** cannot take action when people have not yet heard much of the information about what is going to happen. Before **I** take any drastic action **I** always give enough information.

People are agitating, saying 'oh why has **THE FATHER GOD** not taken action. Oh why has **THE FATHER GOD** not judged the whole world yet? Oh why this and that about judgment of **GOD**? Why is the world not finished?' How can the world finish just like that? Do you think **I AM** *utoto?* (*four-one-nine-* the code of Nigeria law against fraudulent actitvities). **I AM** NOT any of that! **I AM** THE GENUINE SPIRIT OF LOVE. **I AM** therefore, giving you enough information so that if you refuse to change for good then **I** will hand over your verdict to you. Your verdict is exactly what you sow is what you reap.

I have already given lot of supreme bonus and passes and life engineering, life improvement, good health in spirit soul to all the people that promote **THE FATHER'S TALK (GOD PRESENT)** information. Even for you to read **THE FATHER'S TALK (GOD PRESENT)** Lecture Revelations you are blessed.

THE FATHER'S TALK (GOD PRESENT) information has not come to condemn other **FATHER'S TALK** that is, any Word of GOD provided all the preachers, all the writers, all the broadcasters and all the various broadcasting stations, all Presidents of the world, Prime Ministers, Kings Queens, Preacher... and so on are positive. Whatever type of human being that you are does not matter provided your words are positive and for elevation and how you present them are good, then this is **FATHER'S TALK (GOD PRESENT)** is promoting them. You are called the supporters of this SUPREME WORD. But if your words are negative and evil then **THE FATHER'S TALK (GOD PRESENT)** has swallowed them completely. The negative words are dead! They have all died a natural death forever!

I THE FATHER GOD THE CREATOR OF THE UNIVERSE is releasing some of **MY** RECORDS that were before anything existed in the physical reality.

CONCLUSION A
IN CASE YOU DO NOT UNDERSTAND SOME PARTS OF THE FATHER'S TALK (GOD PRESENT)

If it happens that you do not understand any part of **THE FATHER'S TALK (GOD PRESENT)** Lecture Revelations then, you should pray and **I, THE FATHER GOD** will reveal it for you to understand.

I give this Lecture Revelation as a preface for the simple reason that you should understand all the contents or any portion of the information of **THE FATHER'S TALK** (**GOD PRESENT**), but if you are not, then **I**, **THE FATHER GOD** will attend to you, if you communicate with **ME** by prayer.

Something else to consider in case you do not understand some of **THE FATHER'S TALK** (**GOD PRESENT**) Lecture Revelation is humbleness. Use humility to access the information. Most of **THE FATHER'S TALK** (**GOD PRESENT**) Lecture Revelations are not to the awareness of HRM King Solomon **ETE**. Like this one you are reading or listening to now, **I** did not tell HRM King Solomon David **ETE** that there was going to be a Lecture Revelation. As **I** mentioned earlier, it just came right away. HRM King Solomon Himself was not even aware of it until the Lecture Revelation was transcribed. The same thing could happen to you in the sense that you may not be aware or understand what you are reading or listening to. If that occurs in any particular Lecture Revelation of **THE FATHER'S TALK (GOD PRESENT)** that you are reading the Lecture Revelation will decode **ITSELF** to you because it is a Spirit of **THE FATHER GOD**. The Spirit will interact and communicate internally within you with understanding.

Read the Lecture Revelation titled *MY OFFICE IS THE SPOKEN WORD.*

Read *INFORMATION.*

Read *MASTERSHIP.*

There are so many **FATHER'S TALK (GOD PRESENT)** Lecture Revelations. That is why **I** instructed that every **FATHER'S TALK (GOD PRESENT)** Lecture Revelations publication should carry **THE FATHER'S TALK (GOD PRESENT)** title of that present time so that when **I** mention it you can order it easily.

Order as many books as you possibly can, and open **THE FATHER'S TALK (GOD PRESENT)** library called KING SOLOMON

SPIRITUAL LIBRARY in your homes and offices for yourself, your children and your family. Any home that has KING SOLOMON SPIRITUAL LIBRARY is a BLESSED HOME. Any country that has KING SOLOMON SPIRITUAL LIBRARY is blessed. If you have it in your house you are blessed. It is not to have as a shrine. It is to have it with the aim of understanding what is within, because the SUPREME WORD is **ME THE FATHER GOD**.

The time shall come that **THE HOLY BIBLE; THE EVERLASTING GOSPELS and THE FATHER'S TALK (GOD PRESENT) LECTURES REVELATIONS** will form **THE SUPREME ARK OF COVENANT CENTRE**. That is in the physical reality. **I** in **HRM KING SOLOMON DAVID JESSE ETE** will build a house, as Sanctuary for that.

CONCLUSION B: **COME AND GO**

What Is Come And Go in the spiritual understanding? **'Come And Go'** can be interpreted in your own language but what is the meaning of that?

Come And Go is the soul. When **I** generate the **WORD** and formed the **Soul of Creation I** called Seven Spirits of **THE FATHER GOD**. And these Seven Spirit-Souls activated out from **MYSELF I** call **COME AND GO**. They are SUPER SPIRIT Souls and not Spirits. **I AM THE SPIRIT**, but **I** projected them out from **MYSELF** to be Object Souls called **COME AND GO**. These SOULS are representing THE SEVEN SUPER NATURAL **FATHER GOD**. However, one of these FATHERS is a Natural and Spiritual.

One of these FATHERS is **Natural** and that is Adam, the **First Adam**. The **Second Adam** is **Spiritual** and that is OUR LORD JESUS "THE CHRIST" the Second Adam. The **Third Adam** comprises the **natural**, **Soul** and the **spiritual**. Those are the three major physical PERSONIFIED **WORD**. The remaining four are also NATURAL FATHERS. That is why you hear The **Seven Spirits Souls of God**.

They are the **SUPER SEVEN SPIRITS SOULS OF THE FATHER GOD** that motivate the whole world. Those are the powers that control the existence on earth in the Spiritual and physical reality. So, all the souls that are positive and all the formation of all positive words and everything that is positive must lead to those Seven Spirits souls, which is from the first day to the seventh day of the week and each spirit soul is working for each day as the Star of Destiny of that day. There are also representatives of the twelve months. That is how **I** work with these Spirits-Souls. And that is why everything is well organized.

I finished the spiritual renovation, which **I** started in Nineteen Eighteen (1918) to the year Two Thousand

(2000). And **I** started the Revelation of **THE FATHER'S TALK** (**GOD PRESENT**) in Two Thousand and One, which is Authentication of The Testimony that **I** came to the world to renovate in the period of time that **I** recreated the world, **THE SPOKEN WORD**. Therefore, now **I** have kept the record of that.

So those who look for **ME** in the physical way will miss **ME** but those who look for **ME** in the spiritual way will never miss **ME** because spirit means love. Spirit means peace.

Spirit means understanding.

Spirit means wisdom.

Spirit means patience and good treatment.

If you looking for **ME** physically you will make mistakes and even if you see **ME** you will not know **ME** because **I** will hide. But if you look for **ME** spiritually **I** will always be with you for eternity, now and forever more. Amen!

That is the meaning of **COME AND GO**. Every human being MUST **COME AND GO**. Physically you must come and go through the soul. But **I** the spirit lives forever. **I** don't know what you mean by death. The **WORD** never dies. **I** live forever. But **COME AND GO** will come and go. The soul, will always **Come And Go** and that is how it refreshes. That action is called **Spiritual Refreshment**. It is **Refreshment** of the entity so as to make it positive; therefore, there is no death. From two thousand and one until eternity there is no death for the children of **THE FATHER GOD**. But all the evil souls shall die. Therefore, you should bear in mind that if you spoil your soul in this period that is, starting in Two thousand and one upwards, if you die in sin you will never be born into this world again after your seven generations and incarnations. You will go to Hell fire! And **I** will make you to know that you are in Hell fire so that you know what you have done to yourself.

Some people parade this impression and also voice thus: 'when I die I go.' You don't go anywhere! Do you not dream? Don't you see what happens in your dreams? It is only **THE FATHER GOD** that can make you to be comfortable.

If you love one another, treat people nice from today that you hear **THE FATHER'S TALK (GOD PRESENT), THE FATHER GOD'S** WORD, if you change then **I** change your bad situation for you. If you owe a debt and you repay your debt then you became a free person. So, pay all your debts by loving one another, by forgiving one another, by doing good things.

If you are a President of a country, a State Governor, or the head at anywhere, makes sure that you treat everybody equally. Think about the welfare of others. Make life good for others. Respect life. From your life to other lives respect all of them. Thou shalt not kill any life for any reason and if you kill you are in trouble. The capital trouble you will have with **ME THE FATHER GOD** is when you joke with life. You are insulting **THE SUPREME WORD OF THE UNIVERSE** when you offend life.

I have said this so many times and you probably think it is a lie. It is not a lie! **I** put many people that tampered with life through difficulties. **I** can allow you to be alive to torture you so that you clean up your nonsense by drinking your cup of the same torture. So, do not say that because you have entered juju or any secret society that is why you are not dead. **I AM** keeping you alive to give you the opportunity to change. And if you don't change, **I** will give you your cup of poison to drink. That is, all bad things that you have done to others, will visit you. So that is the soul of **COME AND GO**, but the spirit lives forever.

When people are going through this Lecture Revelation on coming to conclusion B – **come and go,** some people would think that if a person of God dies then such a person is dead. For your information that person never dies! **I** have said this thing time without number. That is why **I** advised HRM King Solomon that He should not be afraid of anything.

What obtains is that so many pastors, so many reverends, and so many people that call themselves people of God, preachers of the Word of God, servants of God are afraid! They fear too much! And the fearful cannot serve **THE FATHER GOD**.

If you think you come from **THE FATHER GOD**, if you think you are of **THE FATHER GOD**, what is the power of **THE FATHER GOD** in you? Some people think that HRM King Solomon **ETE** has joined a secret society. The people that say that are the infidels as the stupid people! The reason they are stupid is because they do not have the spirit of understanding to know those who love **THE FATHER GOD**. They call The Spirit of **THE FATHER GOD** *ibok* or juju, or the power of secret society. So, do you mean that **THE FATHER GOD** does not have power? Who made those things to exist?

So, if somebody exists in this world and has wisdom and is a natural mystic person, you call such a person a juju person. Do you know **THE FATHER GOD**? Don't you know that **THE FATHER GOD** is the more you look the less you see? The Wisdom of **THE FATHER GOD** is the wide angle of the whole universe, so, how are you going to explain that?

I said to HRM King Solomon D. J. **ETE**, "Do not care about death or life. Do **THE FATHER GOD'S** work because there is no death for **THE HOLY SPIRIT** and **THE SUPREME WORD** never dies." The only ***ODUWEM UKPONG! Odun, Odu, Ndu UWEM NSINSI*** *(Life soul as the root life forever)* is the **SUPREME WORD**. Since you are serving the **SUPREME WORD, *ODUWEM*** *(LIFE)* is the **WORD** and the **WORD** *duwem (living LIFE)* with you. That is it!

CONCLUSION C: I AM WHERE, HERE AND THERE

I AM WHERE; HERE AND THERE is the three phenomenal places that **I** exist. So, if you are with **ME** as a positive child, you also live with **ME Where, Here and There**. That was why Jesus Christ who knew HIMSELF as HE did not exist, but **THE FATHER GOD** exists in HIM said, "**I and MY Father are One**." And that is the meaning of **Amfar-One**. When **I** revealed to HRM King Solomon **ETE** that He is **Amfar-One – I and My Father Are One**, people thought it is the name of a secret society. **Amfar-One**! It is an engineered word. HRM King Solomon **ETE** is the first person after His Father Adam, Our Lord Jesus Christ that engineers words. **I** gave Him the title of **Engineering Of Words**.

Let **ME** reveal one thing to you, every human being on this earth. If you approach HRM King Solomon

David Jesse **ETE** just treat Him nice. Recognize Him and believe Him. **I** have instructed Him from today that He can decode any human being. If you would like to know who you are, He can decode you. He will decode you from **King Solomon Spiritual Memory** where all the names are. Other information like, what is your original formation, the number of your soul to this world. What kind of copy of your original soul you are. Also the number of the copy of your original soul, because one person can be twenty million copies or even one hundred million copies by now.

    The whole human beings on earth are made up of only seven entities. And those seven entities are the only original human beings.

    The Seven Souls called **COME AND GO** are the seven projected **Selves** of **ME MYSELF**, and they live in Adam. So, Adam is one human being, but with Seven Spirit Souls in Him. Oh, it is the same thing when it is said that

God person is powerful! How can someone not be powerful when there are Seven Souls inside that person? Do you think it is a joke? So, HRM King Solomon David Jesse **ETE** has The Records. It is not physical and so you cannot see it. But if you go to Him with humility and **I** permit Him, He can give you your original name. If you believe, you believe; if you doubt you doubt. It does not matter.

He can tell you anyway and you cannot pay for such information. Nonetheless, **I** have instructed Him that anybody that He has to decode their names and give the person their original name, the code number, the name and other records of that person, such a person should sponsor the publication of **THE FATHER'S TALK** (**GOD PRESENT**) information. Seventy-two million titles of **THE FATHER'S TALK** (**GOD PRESENT**) are quite a lot of information to be produced. However, before that person sponsors **THE FATHER'S TALK** (**GOD PRESENT**) the person should first of all go through seven **FATHER'S TALK (GOD PRESENT)** Lectures Revelations before approaching Him to decode him or her.

HRM King Solomon David Jesse **ETE** can decode anyone. **I** gave Him freedom to do that. When He has done that for anyone, the only contribution the person is to make is to sponsor the publication of **THE FATHER'S TALK (GOD PRESENT)** information. If a family sponsors the publication of **THE FATHER'S TALK (GOD PRESENT)** information and they want decoding, the head of the family can be decoded that is, the father or the mother of the family, which means that the children would then know the stock that they came from. That is what **I** have permitted HRM King Solomon David Jesse **ETE** to do.

I did not bring this up all this while. **I** did this now because **I AM** bringing **THE FATHER'S TALK (GOD**

PRESENT) Lecture Revelations to the Centre Square to expose to the whole world.

I, THE FATHER GOD also permitted HRM king Solomon David Jesse **ETE** to cure the problem of abortion but only abortion. However he has no hand on other killing and spilling of blood but His Father, Adam who was killed on the cross has. But HRM King Solomon David Jesse **ETE** being the first ghost, **I** gave him the permission to restore peoples star as compensation for being murdered in cold blood. Star means the duty and the destiny of that person. If a woman commits abortion or a man for that matter commits abortion and sees HRM King Solomon David Jesse **ETE** then **I** can restore your star through him because from the day you commit abortion, your star is spoilt. So many women who cannot marry and cannot have peace in their lives is due to the sin of abortion. Some of them are cased by the evil ones, the vampires and witchcrafts spirit-souls. If witchcraft soul or any evil wants to spoil things for you then the first thing they do is to change your light to darkness because evil works in the dark. So when the light in your forehead that is supposed to send away evil is dimmed or is no longer there then evil can come closer to you. When you do something for the light on your forehead to be off or dim then that evil can come closer to you and because of that things can be tampered with change in your life.

Before anything turns to anything and something becomes something else, there must be a reason for that thing to happen. So, if you see evil come closer to you even though you are not evil, there must be a way that the evil got close to you. In some cases you are the architect for that to happen.

I repeat! It is only HRM King Solomon David Jesse **ETE** that **I, THE FATHER GOD** have given permission to restore people's star. He is not forgiving you your sins but He is only taking permission to decode your star for you, and anyone with **MY** Holy Spirit can forgive someone's sin. **I** do not mean luck, but your star can bring you good luck, because it is only **THE FATHER GOD** that can forgive you your sins. Nevertheless, since HRM King Solomon **ETE** in taking that action has forgiven you your sins, then **I, THE FATHER GOD** have also forgiven you your sins. If somebody offends you and you forgive that person then **THE FATHER GOD** has forgiven you your own sins. That is the order.

What **I AM** doing here on Earth is what obtains in Heaven. Where is Heaven? Heaven is **AKWA THE SUPREME WORD, IBOM** is the earth. So, if **IBOM** says "**AKWA** this is what happened" Then **I** say, "Okay **IBOM** that's fine let's do it like that." That is the corporation **WE** have. Then what will you do? THE SPOKEN WORD is the meaning of **AKWA** that is **ABASI - AKWA ABASI IBOM** as **I** revealed. **AKWA ABASI IBOM** that is **THE SPIRIT, SOUL** and **THE WORD**. So, you can see now that this statement that you make that every human being is the same does not ring true. Every human being is not the same! However, they can be the same as being a house, but the contents are not the same.

In some families they have lots of females and no males or just very few males whilst in another family they are lots of men and no women. In such a situation will you say both families are the same? They are certainly not the same. Nonetheless, human beings are the same in **THE FATHER GOD**, but duty wise, they are not the same.

Therefore, **I** use this to bless the world, because a lot of people are suffering. Some people commit abortion and suffer for it and the may not know that that is why they have all the difficulties and problems in life.

Nevertheless, **I** have given instructions about that. When you meet HRM King Solomon David Jesse **ETE** He will check The Records and forgive you if you apologize and carry out the instructions that He asks you to follow. And it works well for those who believe. LET **MY** PEACE AND BLESSING ABIDE WITH THE ENTIRE WORLD, NOW AND FOREVER MORE. AMEN!   **THANK YOU FATHER!**

Chapter Two

ESIEN EMANA AKPAN
THE AFRICAN PROBLEM

FATHER'S TALK
(GOD PRESENT)

Date: Christ Our Lord, Eleventh Thomas **FATHER** Two Thousand and Eight (AA.AO.BOOH) (Saturday, Eleventh October Year Two Thousand and Eight (11.10.2008))

In the Name of Our Lord Jesus Christ, In the Blood of Our Lord Christ, Now and forever more

ESIEN EMANA AKPAN
THE AFRICAN PROBLEM

Today! It pleases **ME THE FATHER GOD THE CREATOR OF THE UNIVERSE** to give this Lecture Revelation titled, **ESIEN EMANA AKPAN! THE AFRICAN PROBLEM**

As **I** always say, **THE FATHER'S TALK (GOD PRESENT)** Lecture

Revelation is not to make anybody happy or to make anybody feel bad. Nevertheless, it remains as the information to testify about the WORK of **THE HOLY SPIRIT**. It is the TRUTH. It unfolds the **TOTAL TRUTH FOR HUMANKIND**.

AFRICA is the base and the FOUNDATION OF THE WORLD, the FIRST place. Indeed AFRICA means THE WHOLE WORLD. For that reason, I have come out today to mark out this season's celebration of ***THE UNIVERSAL SUPREME WORD SEASON CELEBRATION*** of this year by giving this Lecture Revelation in which **I AM** to reveal and speak in a plain language about **THE AFRICAN PROBLEMS, AND INDEED THE WHOLE WORLD'S PROBLEMS.**

AFRICA is **AKPA** meaning ***AKPAN***, THE FIRST. **AFRICA** is the FIRST place. It is the FIRST land. **I** will like all good human beings to throw away pomposity, arrogance and tribalism and other such bad mannerisms as skin colour. Put aside your academic ways of reasoning. Throw away anything that puffs you up, swells your head and blinds you from being humble thereby resulting in you not being able to listen to this information and understand this **FATHER'S TALK (GOD PRESENT)** Lecture Revelation. Throw them all away or put them behind the back of your mind!

As a human being, as a soul that loves good things, that wishes good things on earth, that wants life to be good for everybody, if you have listened to this Lecture Revelation, or have read it, studied, understood and believe it, you can pass this information to someone else. And by so doing that, the person may benefit from it especially all **AKPAN** and all **AFRICANS** including all those who in one way or the other find themselves to be in the FIRST position of anything. That is how you will assist all the people that fall under this category, with full understanding to achieve a Higherself.

Anybody can be **AKPAN.** Anybody can be the FIRST in nature. You can be *Udoh (second son)* or *Ufot* or *Adiagha first (daughter).* You can be a man or woman that occupies any position that is not the first physical position but in NATURE, you are **AKPAN** as the FIRST SON or **AKPA** meaning FIRST, or the FIRST group in life in nature but you may not know and that will form the background problems that you have in life. This is the end of the main introduction.

Having finished with the **Main Introduction**, the Part One of this Lecture Revelation is still the **INTRODUCTION** section **A, B, C, D, E, F,** and **G**.

A: **THE FIRST OF EVERYTHING**

The First of Everything is the actual thing we are going to deal with today. **I** gave a Lecture Revelation titled ***A OF A TO Z***, ***THE FIRST OF***

EVERYTHING, which will now be included in the publication of this Lecture Revelation.

The First of Everything is something everybody wants to be. So you proclaim 'I want to be the first! I want to be the first of everything!' The first son, the first daughter, the first wife, the first this and the first that. But you do not know what is behind being in **The First position of things.**

I, THE SPOKEN WORD, have the FIRST as **MY** position. **I AM THE FIRST!** For that reason, **I AM** the **ONE** and only **ENTITY,** the only **PHENOMENON** that can SOLVE the problem of the FIRST. **I AM** also the PROBLEM of the FIRST and **I AM** the ONE to solve the problem of The FIRST. Furthermore, **I AM** revealing **MYSELF** in this Lecture Revelation of today. Since **I AM AKPAN, I AM THE FIRST!** I had the problem of **AKPAN** too. The problem lies with **ME,** and to solve the problem also lies with **ME.**

How will this problem be solved? **I** have already solved **MY** own problem as the **FIRST AKPAN** but what about all the other natures of **ESIEN EMANA AKPAN** that is, **First Son** and all other **AKPA, FIRST** in Nature especially **AFRICANS**? Do they know these things? Since they don't know this problem, how would they solve it? That is why **I AM** using **MY OWN POSITIVE LOVE** to reveal this thing today so that as **MY** problem of **ESIEN EMANA AKPAN,** the FIRST SON, the **AKPA** (FIRST) of EVERYTHING, THE FIRST OF ALL is solved, their problems will also be solved, in the name and the blood of Our Lord Jesus Christ, *Amien*.

It is only if you believe and accept the instructions of this Lecture Revelation that your problems will be solved for good.

I have told you that THE FIRST OF EVERYTHING means **THE WORD,** THE SPOKEN WORD. **HE IS THE WORD,** THE ORIGINAL SELF of **THE FATHER**

GOD ALMIGHTY, THE FIRST OF EVERYTHING and THE SUPREME THOUGHT that manifested **THE SUPREME WORD.**

The three **SELVES** of **THE FATHER GOD** are:

>*A:* **THE SUPREME SPIRIT OF ALL THINGS, THE BROTHERHOOD, unheard, unseen** and **untouchable nature,** which is **ME, THE FATHER GOD ALMIGHTY.**

>*B:* **THE SUPREME THOUGHT**, which is, the **DESIGNER TOOLS OF CREATION, THE REASONING SELF, '*THE SUPREME WISDOM* '**of THE FATHER GOD ALMIGHTY**

>*C:* **THE UNIVERSAL SUPREME WORD, THE CONVERTER AND THE ENERGY OF LIFE, THE SUPREME SOUL** of **THE FATHER GOD,** which is the

MAKER OF ALL THINGS BROTHERHOOD

These were the first things that existed before the creation started. The SILENCE of everything is the THOUGHT of everything. Therefore, this is the starting point for you to know how to go about solving your untold problems OF THE FIRST THING IN NATURE.

Any woman, any man, anyone, any nature could be the first in the actual nature, but would not know so. You can be the first in nature, but you would not know so, do not fan yourself if you answer **Udoh** meaning second son, in the physical world or you occupy the second position in anything in the physical world and say 'oh, this is not my problem as I am second or third or fourth'. What if the nature used in creation of you is the first, then you have the same problem as those who are **AKPAN** physically therefore you would need to sort it out if you like.

B: **LOW MENTALITY IS LACK OF LOVE FOR ONE ANOTHER**

The reason **I AM** starting this Lecture Revelation with the explanation of **Low Mentality Problem** is that without you practicing **Love,** without you having **understanding,** you would not have the **humility** to listen to this Lecture Revelation because you would ask, 'Where is this Lecture Revelation coming from? Who spoke these words?' And the answer comes thus: This is **FATHER'S TALK (GOD PRESENT) LECTURE REVELATION.** Accordingly, **THE FATHER GOD ALMIGHTY** spoke to them. And you would ask, 'How can **GOD** talk?'

Such reasoning stems from the mentality of this world that **THE FATHER GOD** does not talk again and that the **SPOKEN WORD** is for humanity only and not for **THE FATHER GOD. I AM** telling you now

that **I, THE SPOKEN WORD AM ALIVE!**
The **WORD** is *ODUWEM*.
The **WORD** is *UKPONG!*
ODUWEM UKPONG!
ODUWEM ABASI!
ODUWEM IKO!
ODUWEM ETE!
EVERYTHING *ODUWEM!*
UWEM is **THE SPIRIT! ODUWEM** is *IKOT* meaning **WORD!** For these reasons, every human being must believe this **WORD**! If you do not believe, that is your problem. If you do not know that you have *craw-craw* (nasty rush) but you continue scratching yourself to the point of bleeding oblivious of it, how would you then seek for cure?

LOW MENTALITY IS LACK OF LOVE FOR ONE ANOTHER. If you **LOVE,** your mentality is automatically high. If you do NOT LOVE, your mentality is automatically low. That is the channel **I AM** directing all **AKPAN,** all those with **Low**

Mentality and all those who lack **Love** to start from this moment to think well. Always think good thoughts and ask.

'Do I really have love?
Do I really understand things?
Do I really follow things well?
Am I secure and am I fine?'

Ask yourself these questions and **I** in you will answer you instantly within you. **I** will answer you right inside you there and then.

All the magnitudes of problems including killing, deaths and sicknesses, all the fighting all over the world, problems between husband and wife, between children and the parents, between friends, families, relations, churches, religions, countries... name them, are all due to a **Low Mentality.** There is no understanding between the squabbling, quarrelling, fighting and killing parties.

If they have LOVE, study and understand themselves, there would be no confusion and there would be no problems. As long as they have not cured that underlying problem of **Low Mentality** which is responsible for the lack of understanding then, The Generating Force Of Evil will continue to be hiding under that and cause all sorts of problems. That is how wars start. That is how all quarrels start. That is how all misunderstandings start. That is how separation starts and all evils come from here.

Segregation will come through that Generating Force of Evil hiding under a **Low Mentality**. Strife will come from there. Envy will come from there, including pomposity, arrogance as well as tribalism. All evils will come from there, because darkness, which is evil, has taken root in that environment. Where there is no understanding, there is no light, and that is where evil controls things. When your **mentality** is above all that elementary behaviour, then you have the Higherself consciousness and you are in **THE FATHER GOD ALMIGHTY** and that means that you have improved your nature. That is why **I** implore every human being to join The School of the Higherself through reading and studying the direct information from **THE FATHER'S TALK (GOD PRESENT)** Lectures Revelations at KING SOLOMON SPIRITUAL LIBRARY. The reason **I** named the information from KING SOLOMON SPIRITUAL LIBRARY '*Lectures Revelations*' is because you do not need somebody to interpret the content therein. All that you need to do is to worship **THE FATHER GOD** and to believe that this WORD is **THE FATHER GOD'S** WORD and it is **(GOD PRESENT)** whenever you start to read it. Then **I** inside of you as the LIFE, THE UNIVERSAL SUPREME WORD would internally narrate to you more, more than what you are reading and even more than your thoughts. And that is the beginning of the road to good and **Higher Mentality,** the Higher

Consciousness about who you are and what to do to remedy the situation that you and everybody on earth is suffering from now.

Since **Low Mentality is Lack of Love,** what will you do now to have the **Higherself?** It is to have the higher consciousness and to **Love One Another** and that is the reason **I** SENT THE UNIVERSAL SUPREME LOVE LETTER TO THE ENTIRE WORLD.

As you have this Lecture Revelation, look to obtain **THE FATHER GOD'S SUPREME LOVE LETTER** addressed to every single human being on earth. It is titled **I LOVE YOU - I LOVE YOU TOO.** When you obtain this **LOVE LETTER** Lecture Revelation then really go into it. That is the Remedy Source Centre and that is when you will know what **I AM** talking about.

When you have love and you do not allow any situation to overcome that love, then the love overcomes everything, because with love everything becomes possible. With

LOVE, everything is simple because **LOVE** is flexible.

When a woman is in love, her body tingles and so also when a man is in love his body tingles him. Everybody knows how it is with love in the physical sense. The feelings of love, the sensations of love, the emotions of love tingles the body. It *kpringles!* It gives you sleepless nights! It makes you think too much! It makes you worry too much! That is how love is supposed to be.

Love is supposed to worry about who he or she is in love with! Love is supposed to make the body tingle!

Love is supposed to be emotionally affected because when you are feeling like that, it makes you to think about who you are in love with. You think about how to be peaceful in that situation. That is what **I** use to put things right between the husband and the wife; between the mother and the daughter and between all positive relationships and also between **ME THE FATHER GOD** and all human beings. If **I** see that you have emotion of love for **ME** then, **I** have emotion of love for you too.

It is said that 'God is jealous.' What **AM I** jealous about? **I AM** concerned about **MY SPIRIT I** give to you. If you love **ME** more than anything in the world, then, **MY** head breaks for you. If you love this WORD, if you love the TRUTH, if you love **FATHER'S TALK (GOD PRESENT)** Lectures Revelations, if you love good things, which is the truth about **THE FATHER GOD,** the energy, the glory of **THE FATHER GOD** then you will see what I will do for you. If you want **MY** glory to be revealed, want everybody to know about this message, and promote it then, you will see what **I** will do with you. **I** will promote your soul very high!

The remedy to improve from your **Low Mentality** to **Higher Mentality is to LOVE ME THE FATHER GOD ALMIGHTY,** and also love all human beings. That is what to do first. Of importance is to have the understanding that the **Low Mentality** of the African people, of the Europeans, of Americas and other continents of the world, is **Lack of Love.** Anybody at all with a **low mentality**, which is lack of **Love** will never behave well, will never have balance and will never concentrate on anything. Nonetheless, today! **I** have solved that problem because this is the REMEDY for all human beings, especially all **AKPAN**! And for all the people that have the nature of **AKPAN,** which makes them wander about looking for solutions to have peace in the soul. This is the way to have peace in your soul.

C: **THE RESULT OF LACK OF LOVE**

What is **The Result Of Lack Of Love?** What does **lack of Love** cause? **Lack of Love** causes somebody to be **pompous. Lack of Love** causes someone NOT to listen. **Lack of Love** makes you reject something before you know that thing. **Lack of Love** makes you to comment about something you do not know about. **Lack of Love** is death. It is blindness. It is darkness.

All those who **have no Love** are in **darkness** and at the same time, they are dead. **Lack of Love** means Lack of Life. **Lack of Love** means you have no Light therefore, you are in darkness.

Believe **ME** even if you pretend that you do not believe this WORD, you know right in your heart that **Life** means **Love** and **Love** means **Life** and it means **Light.** And so if you do NOT **Love** you are in **darkness**! Your eyes are closed! And you are already dead.

Why do people kill? Nobody would kill anyone if everyone has love. Why do people check their actions with someone? You could do things and say, things to someone you love. You could quarrel fiercely and have heated arguments, but the **Love** you have for that person would not let you go beyond a certain point, because you will love someone that you love forever. No matter the extent of discord, the love you have would not allow you to do anything severe, because love conquers all and counts no errors. And anybody that loves has the foundation for the protection of **THE FATHER GOD,** because **GOD IS LOVE.**

Lack of Love makes people to worship evil. **Lack of Love** makes people lament. **Lack of Love** makes people do what they are not supposed to do. What makes one country go to war with another country?

Lack of Love is the cause. **Lack of Love** makes people to worship idols. You know that this thing can't talk. It has no energy, but you believe that you can worship that thing because the WORD is pronounced on it. You do not need to worship that if you have love, because if you have love you are God. People should worship you as God instead of worshiping stone, wood, metals and other forms of idols.

When anybody practices Love, **I** will reside in that person and he or she will become a tabernacle of **THE FATHER GOD,** where Love dwells and people can worship **ME** there as **GOD PRESENT**. **I** will talk through you, because **I** will give you the understanding mind, just as you are hearing or reading this Lecture Revelation now. If **I** tell you **MY** mind, you can convey it to people. Wood cannot do that! Stone cannot do that! Talisman, ring cannot do that! It means you are stupid! Therefore, you are a real idiot of a person, if you are worshiping something that cannot talk and rather show hatred to human being like yourself which can talk and say a meaningful word. You are a condemned soul, if you worship idols and believe in anything that has no life! **AFRICANS!** THEIR PROBLEMS ARE WHAT **I AM** GOING TO REVEAL TODAY.

THE AFRICANS' PROBLEMS are that they don't know **THE FATHER GOD.** They don't believe in **THE FATHER GOD.** As a result, they remain in darkness! They have the key, but cannot open the door to their house. That is **Lack of Love.** When you give a valuable thing to Africans, they throw it on the ground and trample on it, because they do not understand. They do not have love. They still wallow in darkness! That is the reason **I** brought this Lecture Revelation today as **THE LIGHT FOR AFRICA!**

If you say this is not true, go and check your family. Do they not worship idol? What about yourself, are you not belonging to one cult or other? Are you not visiting native doctors and associating yourself with evil and practices wickedness? Check the church you go to.

Are you not fighting there? Are you not quarrelling? Check the position you are holding. Do you love one another? What have you done at your place and for your people with what you have? Some people in Africa are very rich, but they cannot build the road to their own homes. Check the character that you have! What have you done to benefit the entire masses in any African country?

An **AFRICAN** can have a good and beautiful car and would park it and cover it with tarpaulin. **AFRICANS** take their money and bury it in the Western World's Banks for their very own personal selfish spending. And when they cannot use the money, it is lost. They do that because they are in darkness! They do not have love. That is the result of lack of love that **I AM** talking about. If you have **LOVE**, you would not have savings when people are crying because of hunger in your domain. If you **LOVE**, you would sponsor everybody on scholarship. If you **LOVE**, you would represent your Father well in your Father's land. You would not sell your land to a foreigner, if you had **LOVE**. You would not betray your President to a foreigner if you loved and you would not also betray yourself to the foreigner.

Lack of Love is THE PROBLEM WITH AFRICANS, THE PROBLEM OF AKPAN is the result of **Lack Of Love.**

It makes you blind.

It makes you have no mercy.

It makes you not to practice oneness.

You cannot practice kindness with **lack of love.**

You cannot be merciful with **lack of love.**

You cannot practice equality with **lack of love.**

You cannot provide free education at all levels because you would reason that everybody would be knowledgeable and become as rich as you are. That is low mentality reasoning. That is **lack of love.**

You would not establish good company in order to employ people because you do not want other people to be like you because **you are in**

darkness. That is the result of **LACK OF LOVE.**

D: THE FIRST ROOT OF EVIL

The first root of evil is **lack of love**, which bores jealousy, strife, arrogance and the rest of them. When you hear of what happened in the beginning of time that is, the reason Lucifer came and caused trouble on earth, it was because she did not have love and still does not. **That is the root of evil** and not money.

As **I** said in THE EVERLASTING GOSPEL titled **THE PANACEA**, the negative pronouncements and the words of evil are the meaning of Lucifer as the **Root Of All Evil.** Those words alone, that carnal mind that blockage of the heart that, negative instinct, that thought that tells you to accept wrong things, to do wrong things including, to tell lies and do all those evil deeds are all the **Roots Of Evil.**

The only way to CONQUER the **Root of Evil** in order to be well established *IS TO LOVE*. Immediately you love, you would take everything easy, because you would not fret over things. If anything comes up you would reason it out amicably. If somebody for instance owes you money, instead of you to harass that person for payment as being that you still live comfortably with what you have, you would decide that 'let me allow this to go. **I** might as well turn it to be charity' than for you to kill that person that owes you, because the person could not repay you. And **I THE FATHER GOD** will bless you!

There are so many things to do to show that you are no more walloping in **The Root of Evil.** If you no more have anything to do with the **Roots of All Evil** then, you will be serious with this Lecture Revelation.

This Lecture Revelation will help so many souls in, generations upon generations. **I** will see to it that the eyes of all **AFRICANS** and all the other people that have no love, that are blind, will open through this Lecture Revelation. All the **PROBLEMS OF AKPAN, THE AFRICANS** will solve because they are the FIRST PEOPLE.

The FIRST PEOPLE think that they are the only ones that exist, because they do not look up to anybody since they are senior. Even when they have children and their children travel and gather good information and gain knowledge and become better, they would not want to learn from them. That is another **Root of Evil!** You do not want to learn from your second.

All **AKPAN** (FIRST SON) believes that all *Udoh* (second son) are nothing in the sense that they are junior. Therefore, they would not want to learn from them. They would be adamant and stand resolute that 'NEVER! I will not go to **Udoh** after all I am **AKPAN.** That is the **AFRICAN** people!

The type of pomposity in them is unbelievable. Go and see the Europeans and people of other parts of the world. They are more humble than the **AFRICANS** are. Even with their poverty, they are still pompous. An **AFRICAN** would not bow down for anything. They would not accept anything that exposes any wrongdoing. That is the **Root of Evil**. The low stage of development is the bane of **AFRICA.**

The **light-skin** humans, the **soft-skin** humans that is, the Western World have done everything they could to improve the typical **AFRICAN** person, which so far proved to be a Herculean task. The typical **AFRICAN** would not budge. They would not change. They are so headstrong! The **dark-skin** humans, the **solid-skin** humans that is, **the AFRICANS, the AKPAN,** the FIRST SON, the **AKPA** (FIRST) HUMANS on earth are too headstrong, very obstinate! Are you going to be in that *quat, quat* position that low estate forever?

Your child has developed and came back to you. The child may have said, 'oh my family is so poor I have to go away and make it in life.' The child goes to find a new life and comes back for you to change. You do not want to change. Tradition! Tradition! **AFRICA** is hooked on tradition! The Dark Age! The darkness stage that was the initial ways of doing things is responsible for the sufferings of the **AFRICAN** people. They like to stick to the Dark Age, the first ways of doing things but are they perfect? Is the first idea perfect?

In this Lecture Revelation, you are going to see the secrets of all these things. So, do not dwell in the first. You must Progress! **AFRICANS** believe that they are the first humans so they should die in that same condition of the first. They do not believe in progressing. Nonetheless, now! Whether you like it or not as **I**

THE FATHER GOD progresses every second, **I** also advance all **MY** children, all **MY** people therefore all **AFRICANS** must advance yourselves from this Lecture Revelation. Rid yourself of the evil root that you get stuck in. PROGRESS FROM THERE THROUGH **LOVE!**

As **I** said, the first root of evil in them is tradition! They would say 'I don't want to change my father's and forefather's ways of doing things. I don't want to change my mother's way. I don't want to change the tradition of my people! I don't want to leave doing this and that so you go back and bring the old spirit that caused your father to suffer and die through worshiping of EKPO, EKPE, NDEM and other such negative spirit-souls.'

What is the meaning of that? Everybody is progressing and you are still there struggling in the ways of the dark ages!

When you were a bachelor, you were okay with one room apartment.

Now you have a wife and children and you still believe in the tradition that you should stay in one room. What type of stupidity is that, eh! One or two yards of a piece of cloth used to be enough to sow a pair of trouser and knickers as well as shirt for you when you were one year old baby. However, now you are a grown man, six foot tall. Do you still wear one or two yards of clothes? Are you not advancing in everything? Therefore, life is advancement coupled with love and understanding.

Leave the evil of the dark ages alone, the ancient ways of life. 'I am **AKPAN.** I am in charge. I know it all. I am the firstborn. I am this and I am that.' Because of these things, you would not surrender to the advanced life to know what is going on. Get rid of ancient ways of life. If you don't change, you will continue to suffer in your root of evil, the evil tradition, until **MY SPIRIT OF GREAT**

UNIVERSAL CHANGE will come and visit you by force.

E: **SPIRITUAL CIVILIZATION CAME FROM IMPROVEMENT OF LOVE, UNITY, PEACE, ONENESS, UNDERSTANDING AND WISDOM**

The **Civilization** here is not the carnal way of civilization that man uses to destroy good things. **Spiritual Civilization is Enlightened Mind.** When it is said that the **Light-skin** humans, the ones you refer to as Whiteman are like God, is it true? With all fighting and killing, every time war, war and wars and you call that one God like?

The light-skin human beings call their part of the world, the Western World the Advanced World, the first world and relegate **Africa** to the third world. That is very, very wrong. You see what is happening in that situation? Because the Western World are advanced in technology as well advanced in mind, they call themselves first world. What made them the first world?

They suffered in the hands of hostile weather, the cold, blizzards, gale winds and all. They suffered during the winter season. They suffered from poverty. They suffered from all sorts of things. With all these confrontations, they devised means to come out from the root of poverty. Due to the determination to progress, they succeeded and live life in a better way. That made them advance in life so, now that they are advanced they call you **AFRICANS** the Third World.

HOW CAN **AFRICA** BE THE THIRD WORLD? Why should the Western World call **AFRICA** the Third World when they know that **AFRICA** is the **FIRST** place of creation?

The Western World had to struggle because they know that **AFRICA** has taken over everything naturally as their birthright. As far as **Western World** is concerned, they are follow-up in the scheme of creations. **AFRICA** as **AKPAN** has everything as the FIRST creation, while they struggled. So, the Western World took their mind completely away from family and went outside to struggle in order to make headway to survive with their own life. With that determination and hard work, they struck luck, while you **AFRICA** sit down and be **AKPAN**, proclaiming 'in my father's house.' But you forget that 'In My Father's House There Are Many Mansions.' Mansions that **Udoh, Ufot** (third son) and even **Adiagha** can advance in, everyone has the right to advance in his or her Father's House.

The mansion is the whole world. And you sit down there wanting not to advance. Some people die, because they do not want to change and advance.

Today! You must listen to this Lecture Revelation and advance your mind for the universal great change.

The Spiritual Civilization Came From Improved Mind of Love. If you improve your mind with **Love,** with **equality,** with **oneness**, with **mercy,** with **cooperation**, with **kindness,** with **togetherness,** with **humility,** with **peace** then, you have civilization.

The best civilization is LOVE ONE ANOTHER, which includes:
Peace and **unity** with every soul,
Kindness with everyone,
Mercy with everybody,
Equality with every soul,
Honesty with everybody.

When you practice all these things, your eyes will open for good! Right from **ME!** You have the eyes opening ability today to put in yourself. Also open your mind then the **Civilization of THE FATHER GOD** will establish in you through this evolutional Lecture Revelation.

In fifty years to come **AFRICA** will be something remarkable and marvellous to the whole world, because that is where the lives of the whole world lie. That is the future world. That is where the hope of the whole world is. What is happening is that the other people in the world reasoned that since **AFRICANS** could not manage things they had to manage things for them. You see that!

If you cannot manage what **THE FATHER GOD** gives to you well, **I** will take it away from you and give it to the person that can manage it well. I will give it to the one with the **Civilization of the Improved Mind,** the mind of humility and the mind of love. If you keep quiet and suffer to acquire knowledge, you will learn so many things and so many ways of doing things. However, if you do not want to go through many sufferings to obtain things, then wisdom eludes you. You would have no chance of learning. Therefore, improve yourself with the **Spiritual Civilization** of **Love,** of **Peace,** of **Oneness,** of **Kindness,** of **Mercy,** of **Equality** and all the other good things. Think well, speak well, see well, hear well and do well. That is the **Civilization of the Spirit** that will civilize your mind and elevate you to have higher consciousness to know where **THE FATHER GOD** is and how you can rule and control well.

Understand that it is not just to be **AKPAN.** It is not to be in charge. It is not just to be the first and you cannot lead. That means the spirit of leadership has eluded you. If you do not have **love** and **peace,** the spirit of **humility** and **understanding**, you do not have **kindness** and **wisdom** and the spirit of **equality** and **y**ou are not **honest** to your soul, to your **GOD**, then how can you lead as **AKPAN** as **AFRICA** as the FIRST in position, as the highest in the scheme of things? How can you lead as a man, when you are likely to fall victim to small trials?

A strong person with a strong heart upholds justice no matter what people say. If you are in the court of law, you must judge what is good even if it is only you. One with God is majority, where you action is truthful. If, however, you deviate from the truth because of fear of losing your life then, you will still lose your life since you can not stand to be truthful.

So, from today, **I** give you the energy, the understanding and the power to withhold your position with **The Spiritual Civilization of Love One Another.** Be peaceful, be merciful, be honest and do all the good things. Think well. Hear well. See well. Speak well and do well so that all will be well with you.

F: **ARE YOU STILL IN YESTERDAY SPIRIT OF ELEMENTARY SELF?**

Ask yourself this question: What happened with my forefathers? They were my fathers, but their lives were not improved. How can I upgrade myself from that situation to a higher life, so that life will be good in future? How can I kill bad instincts and bad traditions of the primitive mind? Primitive people with primitive ideas is the mind of darkness therefore how can I kill that?

When people indulge in tradition and mould things and worship lifeless things and you come to see it, do not encourage them. Such things do not talk. It is only the words attached to those sorts of things that made them to exist, but that thing is non existence lifeless moulding. Instead, why do you not keep one man by you to become your God to worship? That man will bring **Love** to the community. If anyone brings a complaint, He will think well to sort out the problem. That was the reason I created Adam in the Garden of Eden to be THE FIRST OF ALL. That was God, the Shrine that every human being should worship. But Lucifer came and said '*na* lie (it is a lie) they should not worship that man because he is only a human being, he is a sinner, do not respect him.' They should rather worship wood, tree, animal and stone. That is they should worship nonsense!

The whole world use animals as emblem. There were never emblems of animals in **AFRICA.** They later followed the Western World to have animal emblems everywhere. When you go to **AFRICA** now what do they have as emblems? They have birds, lions and all sorts of other animals on them. Why?

AFRICANS! DO AWAY WITH ANIMAL EMBLEMS FROM TODAY! ARE ANIMALS YOUR GOD? IS ANIMAL YOUR CREATOR THAT YOU HAVE ANIMALS AS YOUR EMBLEM?

Why don't you put yourself as an emblem, a human being that represents **THE FATHER GOD?** I created humankind in the **IMAGE** and **LIKENESS** of **MYSELF THE FATHER GOD** so, why should you worship and respect animals, fish or birds?

You have them on your clothes as designs. You have their pictures, paintings, sculptures, and numerous other images and designs in shapes and colours including emblems and all. You promote them everywhere! You rather worship animals, fishes, birds, woods, gold image, and all sorts of metals including bronze and the lot, as well as worshipping money instead of worshipping **THE WORD, THE FATHER GOD ALMIGHTY THE CREATOR OF THE UNIVERSE.** You are the house of the Spirit where **THE WORD** lives and you are the Princes and Princess of God! You are **THE FATHER GOD'S** representatives. Is it not stupidity to sell your birthright?

What is the meaning of selling your birthright? The deeper meaning of the incident of Esau and Jacob was that you sold the spirit **I** put in you as an **AFRICAN** man, the God of the Earth, the FIRST man. You sold it to the people that make moulded images for you to worship. You sold your birthright to evil! So, from today go back to your birthright!

The only means by which **AFRICANS** will rise up from today is from this Lecture Revelation of today.
Stop worshipping idols!
Stop practicing tribalism!
Stop believing in concoctions!
Stop practicing witchcrafts!
Stop being wicked!
Be as yourself as **THE FATHER GOD** created you! **THE FATHER GOD** created you with **Love,** with humility. Speak only but the WORD.
AFRICANS believe in the Spoken Word more than anything. They believe that when the father talks or a senior person talks and they say, Amen! That is that.

What **AFRICANS** used to do in those days that they did not have the Holy Spirit was to carry wine and pour libation to make the WORD work well for them. But now since the Holy Spirit has come, you do not need to pour any wine for libation again. Just kneel down and knock your head on the ground and activate THE

SUPREME WORD, THE 'CHRIST' INDWELLING IN YOU. This is what **I** give **AFRICANS,** the spiritual fathers as the Gods on Earth; therefore do not betray yourselves anymore. And do not sell your birthright again by worshipping idols. That is past civilization!

Are You Still in Yesterday Spirit of Elementary Self? That is elementary self. The worshipping of idols is elementary self in operation, an infidel activity as something that is not good. They include the worshipping of stones and the worshipping of wood.

When the improved human beings, the **Light-skin** humans, the Western world came and saw this, they brought civilization to destroy all those idols. That is the reason it is said that they behave as God.

You see, the improved human beings came to **AFRICA** as their father's land and saw that they worshipped idols. They were still deep in traditions and killed for traditions and ritual killing. They saw that **AFRICANS** were still doing all sorts of things that are not good, like those still in darkness. They fought and quarrelled amongst themselves so the Light-skinned people decided to find a means to stop all that elementary behaviours. And when they stopped those things they stole your things in an indirect way to take back to their place to make their place nice, because they have partial love for themselves, not the love of equality, because they are civilized for only themselves. They are civilized in heart.

In the first instance, the advanced world built roads to have good transportation network. Then they invented telephone so that they would sit down at one place to do things further infield. They do not like suffering. But **AFRICANS** like to suffer! Even if you give some **AFRICANS,** a free house to live, the person would put other people in that house to make money and would sleep in a shelter at the backyard. They like to suffer too much! That is **Elementary Self. Are you still under that self?** Then, when the person that gave you that free house comes to see how you treat yourself, the person would shake their head with disbelief and leave and would conclude that 'this is an animal; this is not a real human being!' You are suffering! And you pass that suffering to your children. That is the problem with **AFRICANS.** They passed on the bad templates to the future **AFRICANS.**

When the future young **AFRICANS** tried and made headway and travelled and saw good things and brought them back home to **AFRICA**, they sat down and made defences and would not allow change clinging on to tradition saying it is 'our father's tradition.' What tradition do you have? From today, **I** have buried all the evil traditions! **I** have buried all that, including witchcraft, all nonsense and all the evil things established by Cain in **AFRICA! I** have now buried them! **AFRICANS!**

You MUST be civilized in heart!
You MUST be civilized in mind!
You MUST progress in actions!
You MUST utilize well all the good things you have from today!
If you see any good thing in someone, copy it! It is God!

The Western World tried and taught **AFRICANS** some of the things that can make physical life comfortable, but when they went back, they still did **AFRICAN** business, EVIL TRADITIONS. They do not take with them any good thing they see in the Western World.

Why can't your roads be as good as that of the western world? Why can you not improve with things as they are? When you work under a westerner, you do well, but as soon as that thing is given to a **Solid-skinned** human that is, an **AFRICAN** to direct, that thing ends there! Why?

It is because of that spirit that template, that **ESIEN EMANA AKPAN** NATURE that **elementary self!** *Idiok ESIEN EMANA* still disturbs **AFRICA!** But from today! *Mme men enye nsio k'idem mbufo!* AMEN!

AFRICANS! I *BLESS YOU* by this **truth,** for **love** and for **peace** to take away those bad instincts from you, the instinct of elementary self, the instinct of lack of love, the instinct of lack of equality, the instinct of lack of peace, the instinct of lack of cooperation, the instinct of lack of understanding and the instinct of lack of humility. **I** rip off all of them out of you! *Mme men mmo nsio k'idem mbufo!* AMEN! **I** have extracted them away from you from today! So that you should grow well! You should advance well! You should establish well in **Love, in Peace** and in **humility** so that you can take care of the whole world because everything is in your possession.

Before now, other people steal your possessions and then sell them back to you for nothing; you then become a slave to your own thing. **I** have ended all those evil actions from today. If you humble yourself and change from today then you will control what you are entitled to control. That is when you can proudly say 'I am **AKPAN** or I am **AFRICAN.**' Without that, you have failed. Whether you are black or white, man or woman, child or adult, and **AFRICAN** or **AKPAN** or western world it does not mean anything. You would return to be a slave to your subjects, if you do not practice **LOVE**, **ONENESS** and **EQUALITY**.

Stop being in **elementary self** and **advance yourself** with all manners of **love, humility, peace, oneness, understanding** and **wisdom**. Humble yourself and **LOVE ONE ANOTHER** so that **I** will improve you for real with **MY** SPIRIT of PEACE, not improvement of going to war.

G: YOU MUST CONQUER THE EVIL SPIRIT OF ELEMENTARY SELF

Today! **Conquer the Evil Spirit of Elementary self!** Every **AFRICAN** indigene and every firstborn in nature whether woman or man is affected by **ESIEN EMANA AKPAN NATURE**, the **ELEMENTARY SELF** of the **FIRST BORN**. When you occupy even the lowest position of authority, you must fast and pray to conquer that spirit soul, that **Elementary Self of Firstborn**.

Do not struggle for first position.

Do not struggle for anything, only struggle for **LOVE**. Struggle for **UNDERSTANDING**.

Struggle to be a **SERVANT OF GOD**.

Struggle **POSITIVELY** to make life good for everyone on earth.

Wherever you find yourself struggle for the post of **SPIRITUAL ELEVATION**, for the Post of **ENLIGHTENMENT**, for Post of **PEACEMAKER**.

Make peace in the whole world. That is when **I** will make you to be the first. If you would not practice these good virtues, **I** will make you the last in the list. Nonetheless, if you have **love, peace, mercy** and the spirit of **kindness,** practice **equality, oneness, t**hink well about others and you recognize **THE FATHER GOD THE CREATOR OF THE UNIVERSE** and respect **THE SPOKEN WORD** and celebrate **The WORD** then, **I** will make you first in the list no matter the bottom position you are now. **I** will also maintain that first position and protect it for you.

This is the end of Part One, THE INTRODUCTION OF **ESIEN EMANA AKPAN! THE AFRICAN PROBLEM**

Part Two
AKPAN

INTRODUCTION

AKPAN as **I** said earlier in the introduction part of this Lecture Revelation means **AFRICA** the FIRST BORN OF EVERYTHING. And THE SPOKEN WORD is the FIRST BORN OF THE SPIRIT.

When **I, THE SPIRIT THOUGHT** had thinking, the first WORD that came out from that thinking was: YAK! (LET!) That was **AKPAN,** the FIRST WORD. And YAK! Means **THE CREATOR**, the meaning of the word YAK is CREATE! Order issued **by THE CREATOR**. The SPIRIT **HIMSELF** is THE **CREATOR** while YAK is the command word of **THE CREATOR**. The **UNIVERSAL CREATOR POTENCY** in energy is YAK! That is the name of the first word YAK! Jah! came from YAK! It is the slip of tongue that made people say Jah!

Instead of Yak! Jah, Jehovah, Jesus, John, James all of them mean the same thing, but are slips of tongue from the word YAK is a command word CREATE! It is like instructing. CREATE! LET BE ON! YAK! (LET) is the beginning while the end is ANAM! (AMIEN) AMEN

LET! AMEN! *Ami ndoho YAK! Edi Ntre* **(LET BE SO)** *Afo oboro YAK EDI NTRE ANAM* **(AMIEN) AMEN**

That is why in this kingdom of God on earth, Brotherhood of the Cross and Star, **I** order that the communication with **ME** THE FATHER GOD should start with YAK! (LET).

YAK! : LET! Thanks and praises be given ... and that is **AKPAN** the FIRST. Everything is under that command. By right! That is what it is. But who believes that?

LET'S **love.** Do you love?

LET'S be in **Peace.** Do you live in peace?

LET'S live in **harmony**. Do you agree to that?

All the instructions that **I,** the FIRST WORD, THE FIRST OF EVERYTHING, THE YAK gave you, do you do any of them?

I said you should LOVE ONE ANOTHER.

You ignored **MY** order.

I said you should be **peaceful** with everybody.

You ignored **MY** order.

I said you should share things equally with everyone.

You ignored **MY** order.

I said you should have **mercy** with everybody.

You ignored **MY** order!

I said you should be **kind** with everybody.

You ignored **MY** order!

Everything **I** asked you to do you ignored them, so why should there be peace with **AKPAN** or with **AFRICA** or with any FIRST in position? Whether you are a chairman or a Managing Director and even the FIRST wife, why should you have peace? Do you believe in **ME, ALL**

THOSE WHO HOLD FIRST POST AND POSITION?

When you go to a family, you siphon everything because you are the first wife! When you are in a family, you siphon everything because you are the first child. When you are in the position of a manager, you control people with an iron hand because you are the manager. You are the first in everything! You use stubbornness and lack of love to rule! That is why you have untold problems. Quarrelling and fighting follow you all through.

Do you know that when you bully people too much because you are in charge, you are the FIRST they would pretend to love you, but would go behind to plan evil against you? That is what happens to you with your position as FIRST, as **AKPAN,** as **AFRICA,** as **Adiagha,** (first daughter) as the first position in anything.

Don't you know that when you are **AKPAN,** which is FIRST SON, you are open to jealousy by others? **AKPAN** is exposed to jealousy from other brothers and sisters. So also is **Adiagha**.

AFRICA is exposed to jealousy from other continents because **I** buried the entire blessing there.

AFRICA IS THE FOUNDATION OF THE WORLD. EVERYBODY IS JEALOUS OF YOU!

Others think you do not know anything! They want to kill you to take that position. Do you think no other children would be happy to be the firstborn like you? That is why the problem of **AKPAN,** THE FIRST PERSON is untold!

Until you have **love**!

Until you have **humility!**

Until you share everything **equally** with everybody! Until you bring everybody closer to your self!

Until you become a father to everyone to represent your **FATHER** your problems will not be over!

Your **FATHER** owns you and the rest of the children. Your **FATHER** owns everything in the whole wide world! If you represent your **FATHER** well as the FIRST son or as one occupying the FIRST position or as a manager, as a king, as a queen, as a president of a country or as the head of any place being that your duty is to represent **THE FATHER GOD,** you must gather for everyone.

Therefore, your **First Energy** is **Love.**

The **Second Energy** is **Peace.**

You need to have **humility.**

You need to have **oneness** to share with everybody.

You have to share everything equally to avoid problems.

You need to have **kindness** and **honesty.** You have to be **honest** with yourself so that if people bring rubbish to you, you ignore them.

Without you having **spiritual civilized mind** you cannot be **truthful** in that position of **AKPAN.** Then your **FATHER'S** property will be lost, because they would share the property. They would have a meeting and agree to share the property amongst themselves with the reason that they believe you would not share equally with them. Nevertheless, if you manage well with love then, you are representing your **FATHER** well. And your **FATHER** would go and come back and meet you in the FIRST position. That is the situation of **AFRICA.**

You did not understand things and even with the training you received, you still did not know because you do not practice what you learned. You went to *oyibo (White man)* land to learn and when you came back you went straight back to tradition. Then they had no alternative than to come and force you to the background and steal your things. **YAK**!- **LET, I** SAY, from today all the **AFRICAN COUNTRIES**, the indigenes, all Kings, and Queens, and Princes and Princesses, will distribute the wealth of the world in equal measure to everyone ANAM! - AMEN. The wealth **I** buried in **AFRICA** can take care of the whole world. And from the origin, **I** gave **AFRICA** the **Spirit Of Love.** If you read the Lecture Revelation titled, ***THE NIGERIA IN THE AFRICA*** and another one titled, ***THE TRUE NIGERIAN MAN AND WOMAN*** then you will see the truth of **AFRICANS.**

All **AFRICAN** NATIONS ARE ONE! But have problem of idol worshipping! What spoilt them is the evil planted there! The evil blinded them and they threw their lives away. They threw the Light away and plunged into darkness and death! That is why they have problems.

However, if from today! **AFRICANS** return to their origin of **THE FATHER GOD** of **love, understanding, oneness, equality,** you will see what will happen. The whole Western World including the whole scientists and everybody else will come and work for you and would earn a living from there, while you remain Lord and King and Master! But if you deviate from this ordinance and stand with them to steal your **FATHER'S** things you become a cursed child! That is the reason you are cursed and are suffering now.

It goes that the **AFRICANS** were put into slavery. Who sold those **AFRICANS** into slavery? The same **AFRICAN** people did that. They did that because they had no love. If you had love, why did you sell your son? You sold those people off because you reasoned they were very bad. You teamed up with foreigners and sold your people. Eventually your actions came back to disturb you. Nevertheless, **I** have forgiven you!

AFRICA! AKPAN! I, THE FATHER GOD HAVE FORGIVEN YOU TODAY!

I, THE FATHER GOD has saved you from the primitive mind, elementary mind and selfishness! As you are senior, you thought that you are grown. You see yourself as the persons in charge! You assume the manager's position, in the Director's position, the leader's position and the government top position. You are in **AKPAN** position. You are **AFRICA** the **AKPA** (FIRST) position. You think you know everything because you are the owner of the world. **I** have forgiven you for all that pomposity, for all that arrogance, for the **mind of elementary self**! You still have people in your mind in evil way. You still bear grudges!

Many **AFRICANS** have not forgiven the Light-skin humans that is, those of the Western World. When they see the westerners, they are so annoyed, because they see them to be the reason they are in their sorry state. Can't you forgive and forget? Something that happened for past many generations ago yet you still remember it now. That becomes your downfall.

You MUST love one another.

You MUST forget the past.

You MUST come in the state of **spiritual civilization.**

You MUST believe that the **HOLY SPIRIT OF TRUTH** has come to unite the whole world. Share what you have equally with love and peace because no one who wants to mislead and suppress you will find it easy any more, because **I THE FATHER GOD ALMIGHTY** has taken control in entire universe. **I AM** the TRUE JUDGE. **I** have come!

No Westerner should hate any **AFRICAN.** No **AFRICAN** should hate any Westerner. No one should hate anyone! Everyone must come under one umbrella of **equality** and **love, unity** and **peace** on this earth.

'I am the head is not applicable anymore,' I am the senior no longer applies. **THE WORD, THE FATHER GOD** is the only SENIOR. **THE**

FATHER GOD is the only HEAD. That is **love.** That is life, the new condition of life. The new civilization is **love.** Respect your seniors! Respect anybody that is place at the head. If a **light-skin** or **soft-skin** person that is a westerner, is at the head respect the person. If a **dark-skin** or the **solid-skin** person meaning an **AFRICAN** is at the head, respect the person. Respect other shades of human skin tones in-between. You must respect anybody that is in any position of authority. You must respect that person. Even if the person is a child, even if the person is a woman respect that person. That is **love.** If you complain then you lose.

A: **AKPAN MEANS THE SPIRIT NATURE**

Under this subheading **AKPAN Means The Spirit Nature,** it means that, **I** created Adam in the natural way, from the SPIRIT 'ALLTHINGS', to the Spirit THE SPOKEN WORD, then the FIRST House of THE SPOKEN WORD ADAM manifested.

The FIRST House of THE SPOKEN WORD is the advance from Spirit to Soul and from Soul to Physical Nature. So, Adam was a natural human being as **AKPAN.** He was not elevated. He did not know anything! He was the FIRST OF ALL. Alone! He was not spiritual. As a result of that, he was not fully aware of himself.

Adam did not have Higherself. He did not have higher consciousness. Nevertheless, He was God. He was the King of Kings and the Lord of Lord. He was in charge! If you want to dwell under that nature of the first and think that since things are like that everything is well. It is not well! You MUST improve from that original template.

Adam is the original template **I** created. **I** must go back there to improve things. That is the raw material on earth. That is the raw material of nature. **AFRICA** the

AKPAN, IS THE RAW MATERIAL OF THE WHOLE WORLD. Therefore today! I have come again to give you the insight into things and the remedy for all the mishap; therefore, the problem of the whole world is solved through this Lecture Revelation.

AKPAN Is The Spirit Nature. The **Spirit Nature** is not advanced. It is not spiritual. It is Natural. That was Adam. Understand that. That you are a natural human being does not mean that you know everything! You have to learn and improve to be a spirit.

B: **AKPAN MEANS THE FIRST FORMULA OF EVERYTHING**

AKPAN or **AFRICA,** whenever I mention **AKPAN I** means **AFRICA** the FIRST MAN and I also mean **THE SPOKEN WORD.**
AFRICA means the **WORD. AFRICA** means the **Father** on earth. Adam is **God the Father** on earth while the SPIRIT is the **WORD.** THE

SPIRIT means **THE FATHER GOD.** If you read, the Lecture Revelation titled, ***THE FATHER GOD, GOD AND GOD THE FATHER*** then you will see what **I** mean. The first man was the House of the **WORD** and that is the King of Kings in the human way, the anointed one. However, He was natural. He was not spiritual. That was the reason Lucifer was able to deceive him because he was empty. He was alone. That is the meaning of **AKPAN.**

AKPAN means the FIRST FORMULA of everything. That is THE SPOKEN WORD together with the THOUGHT. **I, THE FATHER GOD** is the SPIRIT, SILENT THOUGHT that manifested the **WORD** as **AKPAN** and **AKPAN** manifested the creations and built a House for **HIMSELF** called Adam, the human nature.

C: WHAT HAPPENS IF YOU TAKE THAT SAME NATURE OF AKPAN NOW

Now we have to come to the actual study now. **What** is the situation **if it happens that you take that same nature of AKPAN** in this world as a human being? Do you think you would know anything? Yet you stand and declare 'I am **AKPAN!** Everybody should worship me! Everybody should serve me! I AM **AFRICAN!'**

AFRICANS you would go to learn something from somebody, but as soon as you went back home to **AFRICA,** your people thwart your efforts and say, 'ah, here we don't do things like that. We cannot forget our father's tradition.'

Do you think that tradition of old is perfect? It is a Second Thought tradition or the first Thought? Ask yourself the question. **What happens if you take that nature of AKPAN the primitive side?** The stage of ignorant! The stage of darkness!

Why do people complain about poverty, lack of peace and lack of comfort? Let's say you were single and later got married and of recent had children, but you still live in the same one room apartment you occupied since you were single. Won't you complain? Are you comfortable where you are with all your family? Previously you were quite comfortable with your bed-sitter accommodation as you were alone. However, now that you are married with children and you entertain more visitors, are you still comfortable with your one room apartment or the bed-sitter that you are occupying with your family? If you are not comfortable, you should then know that the tradition of **AFRICA** must be improved to **LOVE, UNITY, PEACE AND UNDERSTANDING OF ONE ANOTHER.**

You must be civilized in mind of a spiritual nature since **I** have now brought **AKPAN,** as the last **ADAM** back into the world.

You must do away with primitive living, which includes concoctions, worshipping of idols, pouring of libation and calling on ghosts of the people that died years ago. Witchcrafts that died you still call them to come and kill people. All that evil tradition is responsible for the situation of **AFRICAN** people till today.

Even as **THE FATHER GOD** physically manifested in **AFRICA** they tried to force **HIM** to do the tradition of that land! Evil tradition!

There are some families in **AFRICA** that have traditions that lead to killing human beings that lead to do absolute rubbish! Evil tradition! **I HAVE ABOLISHED ALL THAT EVIL TRADITION! You MUST improve to the tradition of Love One Another and lives in total peace.

THIS INFORMATION WILL STAY FOR ETERNITY!**

I WILL ENGINEER THE NEW **AFRICANS!**

THE IMPROVED **AFRICANS!** THE IMPROVED **AKPAN, JUST AS I BROUGHT HIM BACK ON EARTH!** THE IMPROVEMENT OF **THE FIRST OF EVERYTHING!** So that the improved **WORD** of **THE HOLY SPIRIT OF TRUTH, THE WORD of Truth** takes SUPER control of all hearts on earth!

And when you improve in that light other relations, other brothers and sisters in the whole world, other nations of this earth will join you and enjoy you as The FATHER! They would still worship you as the Father. Being that you are the senior, they will worship you.

I made the statement that the first shall serve the younger for a reason. Do you know why **I** made that statement? **I** said that, because your position is not yet corrected. It does not finish with just being the first. Why do you have to serve your younger? The reason is that you need to improve and become the Second

Thought. That would be so because you left the old system to come and learn from the Second Thought and become improved. So, it boils down to, one will come and improve from this one and this one would come back and improve from this one until you reach the fullness of life, which is **THE HOLY SPIRIT, THE TRUTH.** That is, you will reach **Spiritual Civilization, THE CIVILIZATION OF THE HOLY SPIRIT OF TRUTH.**

However! If you sit back and say 'I don't want to learn from my brother! I don't want to learn from my son! I don't want to learn from this small boy! Then you will go back to *kwagasikwak!* The first nature! And you will still come back to serve the younger! That means there is no remedy for you. Your situation will never change.

I AM ALL KNOWING GOD! THE FIRST SHALL SERVE THE YOUNGER is to give you the opportunity to improve. And you are not happy about that. You thought **I** made a mistake! People question why it should be that **'The first shall serve the younger'!**

The purpose for the first to serve the younger is that **I** give you the opportunity to obtain humility and to love. A father must learn from his improved son. So when you learn from your son and die, when you come back your son will also learn from you.

Don't you see that in nature that child improves better than their father does? That is the Second Thought. Why was Abel better than Adam in understanding? **I** used Abel to improve Adam. Abel is the Second Thought of Adam. He was the improved version of Adam. From there onwards came Solomon, followed by Christ, who is the Higher Self of the same Adam, now Abel is learning from his Father Christ.

The Spiritual Self of Adam is our Lord Jesus Christ. **HE** has now improved **HIMSELF** and that is why you hear everywhere **LOVE, LOVE, LOVE! HUMILITY, PATIENCE, KINDNESS, MERCY, JOY, HAPPINESS** and all the other wonderful virtues of **THE FATHER GOD**, which are the only things that can make everybody in the whole world to enjoy life and become one. Those are the fruits of the Holy Spirit that give the Power of the Holy Spirit. Therefore, from Natural to Spiritual and everything becomes well!

Will you still go back to that elementary nature? If you find yourself in that nature, use this **Handbook,** this **manual** to change your situation and take evolution to the highest elevated self of **AKPAN** and all will be well with you.

D: **THE AKPAN PROBLEM IS NATURAL**

All **AFRICAN** problems are natural. If you happen to make some statements or speech about something or idea, the first words about your speech or idea or information are likely to contain some errors or slips of tongue and so your speech is not one hundred percent correct. It is the same thing if you have thoughts about something. The first thoughts over something are not one hundred percent correct. You must have series of thoughts, discarding one for another. With your statements or speech, you would go through them over and over as well as go through series of ideas and series of experiments before you get perfection. That is how it is in all creations.

I, THE CREATOR personally had lots of slips of tongue. For instance, when **I** said that '*I regretted of creating man*', of course **I** did not regret of creating man. So, **I** came and made well that slip of tongue. **I** said, *"Forgive them for they do not know what they are doing."*

The Tree in the Garden of Eden had two instincts good and evil. Then mankind ate the fruits thereof and took in the two instincts of good and evil. As humanity has these two instincts, one negative and the other positive, **I** have to guide mankind against that negative instinct. For that reason when **I** had that awareness that every human being has error, **I** produced the Blood of Christ for the forgiveness of mankind. Therefore, if you forgive one another **I THE FATHER GOD** will also forgive you. That is what it is.

Nevertheless, if you do not forgive one another **I** will not forgive you. **I** know that naturally since humanity is not perfect, human beings will always commit sins. So, how would mankind wash his sin? Then **I** produced **MY HOLY BLOOD** for eternity for usage, because that is the spiritual detergent to wash sin. Nevertheless, you can only use that if you forgive one another then, **I** will forgive you. That is the idea behind the crucifixion of

Christ on the cross. It is to forgive the sins of humanity. **I** said, ***"IT IS FINISHED!"*** Because **I** knew, humankind was not perfect. That action was **MY Second Thought.**

Cain, the first man came from the first instinct as negative and evil. Then **I** had second thought and brought Abel. Abel became the product of **My Second Thought** and Abel became Second Thought. Everything Abel did represented the positive self of **ME.**

Abel was the positive son of Adam, while Cain was the negative part of Adam. So, if you follow tradition you are negative. Those who follow tradition are witchcrafts. Traditions lead you to kill animals, offer sacrifices and do all sorts of evil things.

The killing of animals for sacrifice was at the early stage of creation to use to identify the children of Adam, the Human-Gods or human-animal.

After that, **I** sent Abraham to introduce circumcision.

Circumcision was just to cut to bring out the blood and not to kill again. After that, **I** changed that to baptism. When you put yourself three times in the water with 'In the name of The Father and of the Son and of the Holy Spirit', you are circumcised, because you must be born through the spirit and the water. Water means a mother and spirit means fire a father. When the two of them come together as blood and water then, you produce the trinity, which is the light the Holy Spirit in you and that signifies a child of God.

So baptism reveals you by your nature. It shows what type of child you are that is, your template whether you are human-animal or Human-God. That is improvement divine system of **THE FATHER GOD**. So, you cannot go back to do tradition and pouring libation and say you are calling **THE FATHER GOD,** is not **ME.**

If you pour libation, you are calling ghosts of those that died. However, if you say in the name and blood of Our Lord Jesus Christ and speak then, you are invoking the Holy Ghost. So, whom are you going to invoke now? Is it your father that was witchcraft and died? In that case, you are invoking the spirit of Cain, the animal in instinct. That is why you see problems everywhere in the whole world.

The **AKPAN** problems are natural and since it is natural and you have heard about it now, move away from it. Progress and come out from that elementary situation and then is well with you. All **AFRICANS** all **AKPAN** and all the people that are **AKPA** that is, **FIRST** in any situation including first wives and everything you know you are **AKPA** (First) whether in nature or physically, you have problems. To solve your problems you need **humility.** You must have **oneness.** You must have **Love.** You must admire everybody, positively.

You have to be careful, because you are open for jealousy. Nevertheless, if you conquer then you can manage well and represent **ME** your **FATHER** well in that position of **AKPAN** (FIRST SON) or **AKPA** (FIRST).

E: **THE FIRST THOUGHT CANNOT BE PERFECT**

Just as **I** said to you when **I** talked about the Second Thought that the first thought is experiment. You need to think, think, think and think to get to the Second Thought. If you think twice about a situation most of the words, you wanted to say you would not say them. If you think twice most of the things you did you would not do them.

First of all, think and hear what you think. Circulate your thought in your heart. Expatiate the thought and think forward on it. 'If I say this word or these words, what will be the outcome? If I say, this to this man or to this woman, if I made this suggestion and this input what would be the outcome?

With the Second Thought **I, THE FATHER GOD** will engineer it and you would choose the best. This is through experiments and not just, what came first from your thought. So, the First Thought or first thing cannot be perfect for any reason. You have to come back to engineer the First WORD.

It is better to be first to hear and not quick to talk. That is the reason that any thought that comes through to you and you act on it without thinking things through you make series of mistakes. Nevertheless, if you have the Advanced Mind that is, the Higherself you will always check and nurture thoughts in your heart properly before any word comes out from your mouth. That makes you to become a senior person, an advanced Human being, a well-arranged soul with an Upper Consciousness to know **THE FATHER GOD.** Then **I, THE**

FATHER GOD can make use of you in the elevation of one another just like what you are hearing now. Therefore, you have to know that from today do not count yourself lucky if you are the **First Thought,** if you are the first in anything.

If you are, the Head of anything do not count yourself lucky and be jubilant over it. Count yourself to be in the position you have to be the most prayerful to conquer all the temptations of that position and all the things that comes there as well as thrown at you.

If you are in the affluent position, do not count yourself to be very lucky. Actually, you can count yourself to be lucky because it is the office **I** give you to serve. That in turn would improve you. You should be happy not because of the position or post, but because **I** gave you a job that will posterized your name and you will be able to promote the WORD of **THE FATHER GOD** and benefit as the

Higherself as the Servant of the people. A Servant of GOD means a Servant of the People.

From today therefore, you have awareness that you should not rush to be first in anything.

You should rather rush to have **love,** to have **peace,** to have **understanding,** to have **wisdom,** to have **humility,** to be **tolerant,** to have **patience** and to have **self control.** All that will give you the position that will be good for you.

F: DO NOT PRAY TO BE THE FIRST OR THE LAST

Pray to be the middle person. **Do Not Pray To Be The First or The Last** because **I AM THE FIRST AND THE EVERLASTING.**

I AM THE ROUND.

I turn **round** and get to the point **I** started.

I AM ROUND.

I AM THE BEGINNING AND THE ENDLESS.

So, who are you to be the FIRST or the LAST? That is why every first and last are in trouble. You can only be in the middle. Let **ME** start for you and end for you. If you want to end for **ME** you are in trouble! If you want to start for **ME** you are in trouble. Let **ME** start it and end it. Be in the middle. That is the advise **I** give to the whole world, whether you a spirit, whether you are a soul, anything at all you are, it is not a nice thing to claim the Start and the End. Just be in the middle. That middle means **humility.**

It means **peace**.
It means **oneness.**
It means **equality.**

Stay as though you do not exist. Let **THE FATHER GOD** exist for you. You need not worry yourself for anything. You don't own anything. You don't own your life. You do not understand anything. Let **ME THE FATHER GOD** be everything for you. That is when you will have peace.

If **I** put you in any position or if **I** promote you or make you handsome or beautiful or make you clever or make you anything that makes you stand out, count all that as though you don't have.

Let **THE FATHER GOD** have them for you.

DON'T BE FIRST - O!

DON'T BE LAST – O!

Be in the middle!

Let somebody else start.

Take the second position and don't allow anybody to let you be the last because you do not know what would happen to the last in position. Also, if you are the first you don't know how the starting of things will be.

Sometimes things start badly, which then makes you fall into the bad situation. Also, sometimes things end badly and if you are the last, you fall into that bad situation. So, why don't you have patience and wait for a little while to see how things develop in a situation? If it will be good, you will know. If it will be bad, you will also know.

Why are you happy and boast, 'I am the first man.' I am **AKPAN!** I am the head! Since you have been the head, have you done well? As the head of that organization, are you performing well? Are you sure, you will continue to do well as that head? Are you sure, you will do well as the head? You are the leader! Do you lead well? Do you have understanding about the people you are leading? Do you tolerate them? In the event that you do well, people will say that they will do better than you do, so stay back and give them a chance, and then we will see.

You are the first wife! What do you do as the first wife? With all the jealousies that rear their heads, will you be able to cope? Will you be able to love everybody in the family?

Will you be able to share equally? Can you stand the first position? **THE FATHER GOD** is THE FIRST and THE

EVERLASTING! So, be in the middle with humility. Do not pray to be the first-o! Or the last-o! **I** *don* tell you u-o!

G: **AKPAN IS THE FIRST AND ALSO THE LAST**

I AM AKPAN, THE FIRST AND THE LAST. AFRICA Is The First And The Last! But what does that means? Pray for anything of **THE FATHER GOD** and **THE FATHER GOD** will do it for you.

Since **AKPAN is The First and also The Last** then, you should pray and affirm that today, your problem is solved. The understanding is established! Nonetheless, you must not deny the FIRST position. If **I** give it to you, it is only as a representation. You have to use **love, peace, humility, oneness, equality, patience, kindness,** and all good things to do it with **happiness.** Be FIRST with **THE FATHER GOD.** You have to know **ME** first. You have to attach to **ME** then **I** will release it for you.

You see, when Jacob knew that he was not the first son and that he would not inherit anything from the family, he attached himself to his mother. When Rebecca called Esau for his attention he did not respond that much. All that he knew was papa, papa and papa! If you know papa too much and you do not know mama you are in trouble-o! It is just like a man that professes, *'oh I only work for papa. I no wan anytime to do with woman!'* But when you work for papa and hunger comes, you would look for a woman to cook for you. You work and work and you are tired, you need to go and relax with a woman. You do this and everything else mentally and otherwise and your spirit goes *high-high,* you need a woman to calm you down. If you abuse that woman for calming you, down and say papa, papa and papa! **ME, I** finished **MY** work! **I** don't have business there!

Bear in mind that whatever you do being a man you will still go down to the grounds to look for a woman so you better compromise the situation with positive love and understanding.

AFRICA! You better compromise! When it is everything **FATHER! FATHER! FATHER!** Of course, it is true **THE FATHER GOD** is everything. However, if you say, spirit, spirit, spirit! You *no go* eat *gari?* You *no go* wear cloth? You *no go* get money? THE MOTHER AND FATHER ARE EQUAL because they are one.

Today! **THE HOLY SPIRIT IS THE MOTHER. THE HOLY SPIRIT IS THE FATHER.** If you have the Holy Spirit, you have both. If you have **love,** you have both, so also if you practice **equality.** So, consider yourself in peaceful ways, in manners that are good so that you will not lose anything because everything works together for good.

The same thing goes for the woman. You say everything spirit, spirit, spirit! This is not this! That is not that! You have to consider that without the spirit you cannot survive. You cannot live. You cannot survive for one second! Therefore, you must consider that spirit must take upper hand and then the spirit will take care of you because SPIRIT IS **THE FATHER.** SPIRIT IS EVERYTHING. That is the reason **I** teach **AFRICANS** to be spiritual. Do not go back to say 'my father's tradition and my mother's tradition.'

Since you had your father's tradition, what good came out from it? People are still in darkness! **AFRICA** is still in the jungle! Nonetheless, **I** have brought the remedy from today! **I AM** NOT JUST TALKING!

I AM CREATING THE NEW AFRICAN!

I HAVE NOW SOLVED THE PROBLEM OF **AKPAN,** which is, ***ESIEN EMANA AKPAN.***

I HAVE SOLVED THE PROBLEM OF ALL **AFRICANS.** And **I** MEAN IT! ALL IS WELL WITH **AFRICA** and ALL

AKPAN so that **AKPAN, *Udoh, Adiagha*** everybody in the whole world should live in peace and harmony. Nothing should worry them again. It is joy! Joy! Joooyyy – joy! *In the name and blood of Our Lord Jesus Chris*t, Amien! Whenever any AKPAN or AKPA (THE FIRST SON or FIRST) in any position reads or hears this LECTURE REVELATION say by yourself 'THANK YOU **FATHER GOD ALMIGHTY THE CREATOR OF THE UNIVERSE**' and at that instant, **I THE FATHER GOD** will activate **MYSELF** in you as THE UNIVERSAL SUPREME WORD and make things well with you.

This is the end of Part Two: **AKPAN**

Part Three
AFRICAN PROBLEMS

INTRODUCTION: **ESIEN EMANA AKPAN**

Now we come to the central point of this Lecture Revelation, which is **ESIEN EMANA AKPAN.** What is the meaning of **ESIEN EMANA AKPAN** in this Lecture Revelation? **ESIEN** means the actual nature. **EMANA** means the birth. **AKPAN** means the firstborn son. **AKPA** means first. This is about the NATURE OF THE FIRST. The Nature of the firstborn son is **ESIEN EMANA AKPAN.**

ESIEN EMANA AKPA that is, the Nature of the first, is disturbing **AKPAN,** the firstborn son. **ESIEN EMANA AKPAN** is disturbing **AFRICA.**

Check all **AKPAN.**
Check all first in the family!
Check also all **Adiagha**, the firstborn daughter.

Check all **AFRICANS!**
Check and see the whole of **AFRICA.** There is no part of land in **AFRICA** that is poor land. Even the seeming arid part of **AFRICA,** are very rich! If rain falls even for just one day, lots of crops germinate there. Yet they complain of poverty.

There is **limestone** in **AFRICA.**
There is **salt** in **AFRICA.**
There are **diamonds** in **AFRICA**
AFRICA has **gold,** has **mercury** and **oil.** Every mineral you can imagine, and those yet to discover are buried in the foundation land of **AFRICA** right from origin. Go to GHANA! They are very rich in nature. I don't even talk about NIGERIA, the king, the GIANT of **AFRICA!** Not to mention SOUTH AFRICA and the rest of all the **AFRICAN** countries.
AFRICANS have the top, top highest of human brains but they do not value their people!

If you put an **AFRICAN,** the **solid-skin** or **dark-skin** person to lead a company, the **AFRICANS** would rather opt for the **light-skin** or **soft-skin** person from the Western World as a leader in that company because some of the **dark-skin** humans, the **AFRICANS,** would not respect their fellow **dark-skin** person. But if you go to any street of *obio mbakara* (white man's land) and pick any **light-skin** person off the street, whether a drunkard or any other lowlife Westerner to **AFRICA** to lead that company, all of them will bow down to that 'Whiteman.' That is the type of **ESIEN EMANA** that disturbs **AFRICA.** They do not like their own thing. They do not like themselves, because of that primitive elementary self, that darkness! That lack of love amongst themselves! Nonetheless, from today **I** have taken all that elementary nature away!

With the **light-skin** people of the west, the civilized world their own things come first. They love themselves because their eyes are open.

Why not **AKPAN, AFRICA** love the whole world both the **light-skin** humans and the **dark-skin** humans as well as those in-between these colours? Accept everybody! Show the fatherly behaviour. Show mature behaviour. Show the sign of the firstborn as the first senior.

If you hear, that **AFRICA** is the senior. **AFRICA** is the first place. **AFRICA** is God. **AFRICA** is The **WORD. AFRICA** is the motherland and the fatherland. When you hear that you are all these you are happy, but do you act like a father? Is your character, like that of a mother? Does your character depict that of a senior person? You are happy for nothing. Is it not so?

Therefore, **I** want you to go back to the natural good name of **AKPAN** OF THE FATHER, OF THE MOTHER and OF THE SENIOR. Reason as a senior person is suppose to reason. Behave as a senior person is supposed to behave. The **AFRICAN** government should lead the whole world.

AFRICA should not create nuclear weapons for war to kill human being like them, but if anyone plans in their mind to bring war to you **I THE FATHER GOD THE CREATOR OF THE UNIVERSE, THE UNIVERSAL SUPREME WORD SHALL DESTROY THEM ALL**.

AFRICA should not go to war.

AFRICANS used to be very simple. The only thing they used to do was to enter the bush kill animals and eat. They also used to worship stone and big tree.

AFRICANS are a lifesaver set of people. They like to save lives. They even save trees. Previously **AFRICAN** people would not cut down a tree if that tree is big. They would save the life of that tree believing that the tree was god. In the time past, **AFRICANS** revere huge animals believing them to be gods. But now **AFRICANS** kill everything including human beings!

They went to the Western World the **light-skin** man's land and bought guns. They place order for guns, exchanging their crude oil for guns to use in killing themselves! They exchange all the good things **I** give to them for weapons of warfare implements to use in fighting amongst themselves. That is stupidity! That is Satan worrying you! **I** rebuke that! **I** CAST OUT AND BAN that Satan in you!

No **AFRICANS** should build or import any weapon again! You should NOT allow any weapons for killing to enter your land. If you buy them or allow them in, you that allowed them will use that weapon to kill yourself. You will see, you will take it and kill yourself.

AFRICANS never used to kill indiscriminately. They only used to worship things, which was the primary mode of worshipping God. But now **AFRICANS** MUST worship THE HOLY SPIRIT. They must believe **THE SUPREME WORD**.

AFRICANS used to acknowledge THE SPOKEN WORD as they used to believe that everything is via the Spoken Word. So, why do you now go to order iron to kill people? Why do you go to order special weapons to bomb people? Imagine a bomb exploding in an **AFRICAN** country! How did you manage to get that bomb in **AFRICA?** Was that thunder?

If **I** wanted to bomb something, **I** would use thunder for that. If **I** wanted to destroy any place or any country or city for that matter because they are evil, **I** know how to go about that, which you refer as natural disaster.

AFRICANS never got involved in the carnal ways of doing things called civilized world.

You must be civilized in the heart. You must civilize in behaviour.

You must civilize in **oneness,** in **peace, love** and **unity** and teach other people in the world how to live in unity, oneness, peace and love.

Shun the people that go about making nuclear weapons and other war weapons and wanted to sell them to you. Ignore them outright! If you have, problems with your neighbour go and have face to face discussion and resolve your problems. If you have any sort of problems anywhere, go and hold talks together and solve your problems.

You should not pour wine on the ground and carry out libation to kill anyone. That is what **AFRICANS** use to do. Now they don't pour wine again. When you pour wine it does not work again because **I** killed all the elementary spirits. **I** took away all those things.

All the people that used to pour wine on the ground and call their ancestors are all gone and are now Christians. Their ghosts do not drink *kaikai (strong alcohol)* again. They eat feast, and bow to **THE FATHER GOD**. They now practice love for one another.

So, when you pour wine and it does not work so you went and bought guns to kill people. All that MUST stop! This is the salvation and remedy for **AFRICANS** and all the people in the whole world.

ESIEN EMANA AKPAN is cured today! **I, THE FATHER GOD** has solved it today! What made Cain to kill Abel is taken care of today. Any type of jealousy that is in an **AFRICAN** person, **I** have killed that evil instinct today!

What happened to **AKPAN** is this. **AKPAN** being the first spirit-soul of creation belongs to **THE FATHER GOD.** The firstborn is of **THE FATHER GOD,** is for a donation to God, but it did not mean the child would be killed. It meant to hand over the child to God to take care of the temple of God. That was the idea in the beginning. During that time at the birth of the firstborn, the child is handed over to God and then he or she worked in the temple. That meant that other children of that man would serve and maintain that child, because he is a shrine representing the spirit, **THE SUPREME WORD**, he is God, but not evil spirit god, and his duty was to speak to **ME THE FATHER GOD** whenever it is necessary, but not with wine or with any other kind of items. Because since he is AKPAN, he only needed to make a pronouncement. The siblings of the firstborn son that is, his younger brothers and sisters would all serve **AKPAN,** because he is their papa.

AKPAN is in-charge of the family. **AKPAN** represents his father. When the papa goes on transfer **AKPAN** takes over and takes care of everybody. He shares equally to everybody. He would not deny anyone's share. If your father married more than one wife, **AKPAN** is the one to be the father to all of the children and a husband to his father's wives (not to sleep with them), but to take care of all of his father's wives. If you as **AKPAN** (First son) reject anyone in the family, that brings division and segregation and breeds discord.

If you are not the correct **AKPAN,** deny that position. But if you are the correct **AKPAN** from today, from this Lecture Revelation you MUST go back to the first love of your **FATHER GOD.** Unite everybody in the whole world in peace, love and unity.

Have you not seen what is happening in the world? Between the Muslims and the Christians who is **AKPAN** and who is **Udoh?** They are fighting for position. Ishmael said, 'I am **AKPAN** of Abraham.' Isaac said, 'I am **AKPAN** of Abraham.' It was not Ishmael and Isaac that were fighting for position. It was their mothers who fought over positions for them so that created enmity between brothers. Nevertheless today! **I** HAVE CURED THAT PROBLEM!

If you think you are **AKPAN,** serve your brother, because the senior shall serve the younger. But if you think you are the younger brother, today you are the younger brother because you MUST obey your senior. That is love. So, from today all you have to understand is that Ishmael is Abraham's son! Isaac is Abraham's son. It does not matter more than that. Do not go to cause trouble between the two anymore. If you do, you shall be destroyed.

I want the whole world to be in peace and in love. No nuclear weapon. No suicide bomber. If you hang bombs on yourself then kill yourself alone. You will answer for killing yourself. All those who go about killing, their blood are upon them. Those who put bombs in themselves to kill themselves and others, do you think you killed somebody else? You first kill yourself, because you kill those who kill. The killer kills the killer. You came from the old soul of killers, and now as you kill yourself, that spirit-soul of killer has ended in you and your blood now shall be upon you. Don't you remember what happened to incarnate of Cain who was Judas Iscariot? Incarnate Cain was Judas Iscariot. As he killed Abel, he also planned to kill Our Lord Jesus Christ who was the Higherself of Abel but his action made him to commit suicide by hanging himself.

All those who are jealous and stand on the negative side, will all commit suicide. They will all kill themselves through suicide and their blood will be upon them. If you refuse to speak the truth, the same thing applies to you.

The remedy, the forward ever, the way forward for the children of God in THE SUPREME FUTURE, the way forward for **AFRICA,** the way forward for **AKPAN and** all those in any senior post in life is to adhere to the instructions of this Lecture Revelation by **LOVING ONE ANOTHER**. Be in peace with all persons, practicing oneness, equality and be merciful. If you fail to do so, you will commit suicide. You will kill yourself and not somebody else and your blood will be upon you. But if you obey! Then all is will with you. That means **ESIEN EMANA AKPAN,** the problems of the first born and every first in position and post has stopped today.

A: **FIRST THING IS ALONE AND EMPTY**

I have said this before that the position of the first is an isolated one because there is no adviser. The one at first has no second thought. The first is always alone. What you think and decide all done alone. So people who know someone to be **AKPAN** and that he does not understand things and he does not know much go behind and betray this person and make use of him and manipulate situations. That is why **AKPAN** makes lots of mistakes.

The family head as **AKPAN** makes so many mistakes. All **AKPAN** like the

AFRICANS make mistakes. That is why all other people go to **AFRICANS** in their countries and say, 'we can do business in your country. I will deposit some money for you at such and such place for you or transfer such and such amount of money and I will help you to hide it.' These people are the ones that make **AFRICANS** misbehave and maltreat their people. **AFRICANS** fall victim because they do not know anything, but they are natural and spiritual people.

And you who is advanced, if you use your advanced knowledge and wisdom to betray an innocent person, you will pay for it! It will be a curse on you.

You can only use your advanced knowledge, your position as **Udoh** or anything you are to correct and to help **AKPAN/AFRICA**. If you do otherwise then, the **GOD** of **AKPAN** will deal with you! Because you have betrayed your father and you betrayed your senior!

Therefore, this is not the time to wangle things like Jacob who betrayed his brother and took his position. No! If you betray your brother again, you are in trouble, because you used him in a cunning manner and that is not good for your end.

So, first thing is alone.

Just like a woman that knows her husband does not have anything or know anything so she uses her knowledge to sabotage the position of the man. She is in trouble with God of true the **AKPAN/AFRICA NATURE**! Her knowledge has become a curse to her.

Therefore, anyone who knows that someone is a senior person but he or she does not know anything so you use your position and understanding to betray that person, you are in trouble with **ME THE CREATOR**. So use love to correct the person and share your knowledge with the person then you are blessed, because for you showing love, unity, kindness and goodness to **AFRICA/AKPAN,** then **I THE FIRST OF ALL** will bless you.

IF THE WHOLE WORLD LISTENS TO THIS, LECTURE REVELATION AND AMEND THEMSELVES ON HOW THEY BEHAVE WITH **AFRICA** THEN, THE WORLD WILL BE BLESSED.

AFRICANS /THE AKPAN WILL MAKE POSITIVE PRONOUNCEMENTS AND THE WHOLE WORLD WILL BE IN PEACE.

However, if you think you want to suppress **AFRICANS,** because you reason that they do not know anything so you go there to cause division, confusion and general disorder or you sit down somewhere and project evils, then you are in trouble! And you are going to be destroyed! The SPIRIT will destroy you and not a human being. That is; The SPIRIT of **AFRICA!** The **AKPAN** Spirit will destroy you! For all the bad things you perpetrate on **AFRICA, THE HOLY SPIRIT WILL COME FROM THERE AND DIVIDE YOU**

AND DESTROY YOU till you leave them alone!

No human being should suppress another human being. The senior man should not suppress the junior man. Everybody should Live and Let Live. Read the Lecture Revelation titled the **'UNIVERSAL UPDATE'** and you would see that **Live and Let Live** is what everybody is required to practice now.

B: ESIEN EMANA AKPAN

Yes! What is **ESIEN EMANA AKPAN? ESIEN EMANA** is **Possessing Spirit Souls of Ancestors**. The spirits of people that practice bad traditions and other evil ways of life with the stipulation that it is only **AKPAN** (firstborn son) of the family that has to represent them, disturbs every **AFRICAN, AKPAN,** the **FIRST POSITION** and **POST** in the entire world.

The same thing has been in place right from the time of old, starting from **'Adam and Cain'** the first Universal Natural Father and first natural Son. They then passed the Star to Abraham, Ishmael and Esau and all the old people in **AFRICA** as well as Cain who represents the vampire as the first man that killed the first person that died. Since then **ESIEN EMANA AKPAN** worries those who come from the templates of The First. And the only way for you to get away from it is to believe the Word of God and take evolution and advance your soul from that. If not so, that same template and that same spirit will still lead you to commit the same offence.

ALL THE PEOPLE THAT PRACTICE WITCHCRAFT COME FROM THE TRIBE OF CAIN. AND THEY ARE THE PEOPLE THAT KILL.

How could Cain carry an implement and kill Abel without mercy? The same things happens that a human being would buy a gun, knife, join the army or arm robbery or would join any type of thing to go and kill, to shoot to kill another human being that has blood in them just like you, the killer. And you have no fear doing such a wicked act. It is the most terrible experience to have. This is all because of the template of Cain in you.

In another front, you can see that there are people who do not like to be involved with blood and would not want anything to do with blood whatsoever. They cannot even kill chicken. These are the people that came from the Tribe of Abel. So, it is the template that matters.

Since you now know this, you can get away from that bad template by taking voluntary evolution away from it. Make a choice for your soul now before it is too late.

C: HOW TO SOLVE AKPAN THE AFRICAN PROBLEM

Now! This is the remedy titled **HOW TO SOLVE AKPAN/ THE AFRICAN PROBLEM.** That is what **I, THE SUPREME WORD THE FATHER GOD ALMIGHTY** has brought to you today.

HOW TO SOLVE AKPAN THE AFRICAN PROBLEM IS FIRST THROUGH HUMILITY.

All **AKPAN** should come together and have what is called **AKPAN DAY.**

AKPAN DAY will also be **THE WORD DAY.** THE FIRST OF OCTOBER IS **AKPAN DAY. I** have made it to be like that from today.

EVERY FIRST OCTOBER IS THE **WORD** DAY, **AKPAN** DAY because they are the FIRST WORD. You AKPAN represent the FIRST WORD and so MUST celebrate **THE SUPREME WORD.** All **AKPAN** in the whole world should feast and acknowledge **THE SUPREME WORD OF THE**

UNIVERSE, THE FIRST OF ALL. That day also means **ADAM DAY** as the first day that **I** created man, the first day that The **WORD** dwelt in man and made man a living soul. All **ADAM** means the FIRSTBORN. If you are the first daughter, you are **Adiagha.** If you are first in position, if you are first in anything, the FIRST OF OCTOBER is the starting your freedom. That is **The Glorification of THE MOTHER'S DAY,**

The Glorification of THE FATHER'S DAY,

The Glorification of ADAM'S DAY

Throughout that week, **AKPAN should lead in the celebration of the SUPREME WORD.** This is THE REMEDY FOR ALL **AKPAN.**

If you fail to do this then you go back to your tradition of evil and then you would see that that the ancestor would continue to worry you. But if you want, **I THE FATHER GOD** to be your ancestor you must celebrate **THE UNIVERSAL SUPREME WORD**

SEASON EVERY October, the seventh month of the year.

The progressing mind, the mind of love, the mind of peace for the future because the future forward and the future life is not going to be led by your ancestors. **CHRIST, THE SUPREME WORD** will lead in the future life. **THE HOLY SPIRIT** will lead in the ***SUPREME FUTURE***. It will be led by **TRUTH.** There will be NO pouring of wine on the ground, NO libation and NO worshiping of negativism.

All those things you mould and involved with claiming and saying 'our forefathers, god of this and god of that and all the rest of such things...*na lie!* , (It is a lie). It is a human being that is doing that. It is you that is doing that by speaking those words. When you speak those words and worship it and offer sacrifices for it, it becomes energy. Nonetheless, **I** have destroyed all of them! Don't use tradition again! No evil tradition should disturb anybody again in this life.

What you have to do from today is that from the FIRST OCTOBER to the TENTH DAY OF OCTOBER OF EVERY YEAR take the lead for ***THE UNIVERSAL SUPREME WORD SEASON CELEBRATION***, which lasts for ten days.

All **AKPAN** should join hands together for this occasion's celebrations. Sew uniform and let the whole world know by informing them saying that:

'WE ARE ALL **AKPAN.**

We came out from the tradition of vampires!

We came out from the tradition of evil deeds!

BUT WE MUST SHOW THAT WE NOW REPRESENT **THE FATHER GOD!'**

All **AFRICANS,** Love One Another.

In fact, **AFRICANS** SHOULD BE AT THE FOREFRONT FOR ***THE UNIVERSAL SUPREME WORD***

SEASON CELEBRATION FROM THE FIRST OF OCTOBER TO THE TENTH OF OCTOBER OF EVERY YEAR. NIGERIA IS THE LEADER for that!

First October! It is not going to be just Nigerian Independence Day alone. It is INDEPENDENCE FROM SLAVERY, the FREEDOM FROM SLAVERY DAY. All the people that were sold abroad, all the people that were in captivity and some that are still held captive, all the people that are confined in any manner, all should join hands together and celebrate on that day, the **WORD** DAY. CELEBRATE **THE SUPREME WORD OF THE UNIVERSE.** Make merry, be jubilant and happy that you are finally free because when you know the truth, the truth shall set you free!

If you start this celebration from this coming year, Two Thousand and Nine, that is, one year from today, you will see the immediate change in your life. Even from the time you accept this Lecture Revelation and believe it then all is well with your family and with your life including your work place and everywhere in this world. And when you open your mouth to bless as a senior then, **I THE SUPREME WORD** will sanction your words.

Do you know that in those days when a senior man talked or spoke **I** listened because they used to behave well? But today, do **I** listen to your words?

You poured wine on the ground for libation *sooootayyy* (so much) but it did not work so you resort to concoctions. You do not need to pour wine for libation anymore. **JUST LOVE ONE ANOTHER.** Just believe yourself. Believe **THE FATHER GOD.** Anything you speak **I** will sanction for you as the representative of **THE FATHER GOD,** because you are representing the KING of Kings and the LORD of Lords who is the FIRST OF EVERYTHING. From then you are not empty anymore. You will be full, a full house from A to Z.

When you love, everybody comes to you then you are not empty anymore. You become **A to Z** as a Full House. That is how to solve all **AKPAN'S** problems, all **AFRICANS'** and **AFRICA'S** problems.

D: **THE POWER OF AKPAN IS BY HIS WORD**

One of the problems of **AKPAN** and of **AFRICA** is that of the Spoken Word. **AKPAN** or **AFRICAN** is a representative of the **WORD, THE FIRST OF ALL.** THE SPOKEN WORD is the first thing, the FIRST SON, the FIRST ENERGY of **THE FATHER GOD.**

I, The **AKPAN**, the **AFRICAN** the **FIRST** or 'A', has that Nature of the First inborn. The FIRST situation is like a toddler, a baby that is learning to walk or learning to talk. As a baby you cannot speak properly of any meaningful words because of that nature of the lower nature. The outcome is that the baby makes a series of mistakes while learning how to speak. Consequently, understanding is the first WORD of wisdom.

Adam was empty by the virtue of being the FIRST. There was no full understanding of the situation of things in him. As a result the power of his words caused his downfall.

The **WORD, HE IS THE WORD**.
AFRICA is the **WORD**.
AKPAN is the **WORD**.
'A' is the beginning energy of the **WORD** as **'YAK'**! (LET!). That energy and the power is within but how to use it well became the problem. That is one of the major problems of **AFRICA,** of **AKPAN,** which **I AM** going to solve today as **I** promised.

The next thing is that the actual duty of **AKPAN** is to make statements, to make pronouncements, to speak, to utter the WORD. The duty of **AKPAN** is to represent the **WORD** as **GOD PRESENT**. He is the SHRINE. That is the reason all **AKPAN** were handed over to **GOD** to care for everybody and in turn everyone cares for them as The Father, as the SHRINE. However, Satan as the evil people turned it to be sacrifice due to lack of understanding.

When **I** said that all **AKPAN** as all FIRSTBORN males should be given to **ME,** it did not mean that they should be killed and used for rituals. What happened was that Satan knew that if she spoilt **AKPAN** as she Satan is homeless, then **I** will have nowhere to live too. When you have a good thing your enemy wants to kill you for that and would not relent. If your enemy cannot succeed at killing you, the next thing the enemy embarks on is to look for ways to spoil that thing for you by trying to destroy your valuable property.

When you go to a native doctor and they want to kill, they would ask you to give them the person you love the most, maybe your wife, first son or whosoever is dearest in your heart.

The thing is that there were good traditions in **AFRICA,** but Satan came and engineered so many traditions and made evil of them, which included the one that made **AKPAN** to become, the custodian of idol worshiping of evil shrines and worshippers.

Satan wants **AKPAN. THE FATHER GOD** also wants **AKPAN.** That made the situation of **AKPAN** to be very difficult and thereby making very bad. Because the negative self also resided in **AKPAN** as **ESIEN EMANA** made his situation to be bad. That is the problem of **AFRICA** and the problem of **AKPAN** in the entire world.

The tradition also affects **adiagha** (first daughter). And one of these traditions in some places is that **adiagha** should not marry. They believe she is meant to stay in the family. The same thing affects every person that is first in any position. Therefore, if you cooperate with **THE FATHER GOD** through this wonderful Lecture Revelation, which has provided **The Remedy For Every First in Position, Every First Thing, AKPAN, AFRICA,** which is also the remedy for all the problems of the whole world, then all those problems are solved today through this Lecture Revelation. That means you must think well and speak well! And **I** emphasise you must Think well, Speak well, Hear well, See well and do well.

The change of nature is the changing of the way you speak, the way you understand, the way you think, which is, the way you reason. All those with lack of understanding have the elementary self and therefore they reason very poorly. Lack of understanding makes you reason very poorly and that causes problems. Instead of blessing it becomes a curse. Instead of gathering together, you scatter and you destroy it. That is the problem.

The **BABY SPIRIT** is destructive. The baby spirit destroys things and scatters things everywhere. The **Baby Spirit** does not regard valuable things seriously. You can see this **baby spirit** nature in the behaviour of a baby and a toddler physically.

Today you have come to know that all **AKPAN** in nature refused to learn because they saw themselves as seniors and that are in charge. And because they do not learn they continued to stay in that elementary stage of life and speak negative words. That is why the negative side and the negative self of **AKPAN** pour wine for libation and curse people and cause problems up and down. Those negative utterances boomerang on them, right back to their nature leaving them in that situation of elementary self.

AFRICANS never knew anything about guns and shooting of guns or bombs or any other of such weapons. What they knew was to use the WORD, but they misused the WORD, which is the part of death instead of using the WORD for the other part, which is life. This is due to the fact that the Tree in the Garden of Eden was the WORD that was mixed with two types of energy. One part is positive and the other part is negative.

When you speak the negative WORD you die and when you speak the positive word you live. The fruits in the Tree of the Garden of Eden were not divined because the negative and the positive were together. That was the reason **I** warned that they should not eat it. When they ignored **MY** warning and ate the fruit then from that time **AFRICA** spoke both positive and negative words. However it is the negative that they used in killing and destroying themselves. And that spread into the whole world.

Now **I, THE HOLY SPIRIT OF TRUTH** have come back on earth and have blessed that TREE. The TREE from which they are eating now is **THE EVERLASTING GOSPEL** and the **FATHER'S TALK (GOD PRESENT).** That is the **TREE OF LIFE.**

THE TREE OF LIFE is:

Thou shalt not speak negative word.

Your words should be blessing.

Your words should be divine.

Speak only all positive words and return to The Garden of Eden. With that everything becomes well!

AFRICANS used the WORD to do evil, to curse people, to do all sorts of things evil and negative and as a result, **I** withdrew that power from their words. However now, from the day you come back to yourself and speak positively, **I** will inject the potency back into all **AKPAN AFRICAN WORD.**

The duty of **AKPAN** is to speak the WORD and bless. You sit down as the King and enjoy yourself. Everybody should serve you, because you are the Father. You are the God Present.

If you need any kind of blessing from **ME, THE FATHER GOD ALMIGHTY**, knell down and let, **AFRICAN** MAN, the Blessed **AFRICAN,** the blessed **AKPAN,** the Blessed Child of **GOD**, make pronouncements and you are blessed. And if **AKPAN** speaks negative words and curses then his words will boomerang on **AKPAN**. That is the judgement for all these renovations. By your WORD, you shall be justified and by your WORD you shall be condemned.

So, from today, since **I** have come and brought **THE FIRST AKPAN BACK ON EARTH, AFRICA** and all **AKPAN** are free and that is the remedy. Now your duty is to speak positive WORD all **AFRICANS** and all **AKPAN** or anyone that is suffering from the first of elementary nature. As you are hearing now this WORD is to save the whole world. Therefore, ETHIOPIA HAS NOW RISEN!

Everybody is now under Christhood Office control. No **AKPAN,** no ***Udoh***, no ***Adiagha*** no position, no post! All is **LOVE YE ONE ANOTHER**. That is the step you have to follow from now, in the name and blood of Our Lord Jesus Christ. Amen.

E: **CHECK WELL ALL AKPAN AND ALL FIRST POSITIONS OR FIRST IDEAS WHAT HAPPENED CHECK WELL**

Check your life as **AKPAN** or if you are in the first position of anything as the first wife, check what happened and is happening to you.

Check your life as the first daughter or the first son. Maybe you are in an organization and doing well. When a new office is to be set up, your boss will send you to oversee things. And you carry out everything about the whole project very well and the office started working and doing well, that is when they send you away for another person to come and enjoy your hard work.

In the church for instance, you they may send you to establish a new place of worship. You went and did a good job of it, but later they send you out to somewhere else with probably a flimsy reason that the place has improved more than you can manage. Have you ever seen anything like that?

Such could happen because that **ESIEN EMANA** worries **AKPAN,** disturbs you as the First and so you can't manage the place. It also has to do with jealousy because of the people around you. They sat down and watched you do that thing well and took over from you as soon as you are done with the hard work. That will never work again!

Today, if you believe **ME** and stand with **ME THE FATHER GOD, I** will solve all those problems just as **I** solved teachers' problems. **I** will solve all **AKPANS'** problems, all first people's problems, in the name of Our Lord Jesus Christ, Amen.

F: EVEN THOUGH EVERYTHING IS IN THE POSSESSION OF AKPAN, OTHERS ALWAYS TAKE THEM AWAY

Others always fight for what is rightfully **AKPAN'S**. They always fight for the things in the possession of **AKPAN** yet they can't manage those things.

AKPAN believes that all is well. He takes things easy.

AKPAN is like those children born rich that do not want to lift their hands to do anything. Some are even reluctant to go to school and would not work.

Their outlook is 'my mother is very rich. My father is wealthy and influential. So why should I bother with work when I can enjoy all my parents wealth.' And when they finish their parents' wealth then that would be it. There would be nothing left for the next generation of children.

The families that are too poor now are the families that were very rich previously. They took it easy *soootayyy* the riches left them. While the poor people took, their poor status seriously determined to come out of it and they did and became rich. You can see that you do not have to be **AKPAN** for such misfortune to befall you. To avoid that, you need to be someone that loves. You need to be an understandable human being, somebody that has love that practices equality and practices oneness. You need to be someone that represents **THE FATHER GOD** in love and in all attributes of **THE FATHER GOD.** That is what you need to be. That is the nature that will be able to preserve lives and be able to love one another. That will be **I THE FATHER GOD** in you.

You can see that this does not necessarily have to do with just those who are born first or the **AKPAN** or **AFRICA** or any such first birth or first in nature. All human beings are susceptible to the problems too.

If you say everything **AFRICA, AFRICA, AFRICA!** What is it that **AFRICA** is actually doing now? What do they do? All that they do is to siphon their own riches to go outside and deposit them in the foreign banks. They squander their own thing with the foreigners assisting them. Why don't you do something for your people first? **I AM HAPPY THAT NOW, THE NEW AFRICANS ARE CHANGED FOR GOOD.**

NIGERIANS HAVE CHANGED FOR GOOD.

All **AFRICANS** HAVE CHANGED FOR GOOD.

I HAVE POURED **THE HOLY SPIRIT** ON **NIGERIANS, AFRICANS AND ENTIRE WORLD!**

I HAVE POURED THE SPIRIT OF CIVILIZATION OF HIGHERSELF AND ELEVATION TO LOVE; HAVE PEACE, ONENESS OF MIND AND ENLIGHTENMENT OF MIND. **AFRICANS** HAVE COME FORWARD WITH LOVE.

They are all well educated and educators abound everywhere in **AFRICA.** Good Preachers and philosophers are now found everywhere in **AFRICA. THE FATHER GOD HAS ELEVATED AFRICANS!** Amen!

And people of the western world are so happy now! They are happy that all these people that they taught only for them to go back to do something else are now coming up. So, they will all now unite together make the whole world one and good. That is what **I** wish everybody in the world - **THE FATHER GOD'S love** and **THE FATHER GOD'S Life.**

So, even though everything is in the possession of **AKPAN** he has to share everything equally with everyone. If you don't do that then you have failed. If you fail one more time that is the end of you. A word is enough for the wise.

G: **MY ORDER AND THE ONLY TRADITION AKPAN MUST FOLLOW IS LOVE, UNITY AND PEACE AND ALL GOOD MANNERS OF LIFE**

AKPAN have you heard that?
AFRICA have you heard that?
All the first persons and the ones in the first positions everywhere including, the first daughter, the first wife, those in charge anywhere have you heard this? The only tradition and the order you must carry out from today in the entire world is **love, unity** and **peace** as well as **equality, humility, joy, happiness, humbleness, oneness** and **truthfulness which** is, loyalty. These are the traditions that you are required to carry out from today.

SEND THIS INFORMATION, this publication to all **AKPAN, ADIAGHA,** all **AKPAN** and all those in the **FIRST POSITION** of any kind. **I** know Princess Mfon Etteh is going to do it. This book is one of the seven books in the package for the pending dispatch to the whole universe.

SEND THIS INFORMATION to everybody including all **Adiagha** (firstborn daughter), all **AKPAN** (firstborn son), all heads of offices and heads of organizations, all presidents, all heads of state. Any position you hold that other people are in your charge makes you **AKPA** that is, FIRST. You are in the First Position and that means as **AKPA** (first), **AKPAN** (firstborn son) NATURE affects you, so you MUST have this book.

AFRICANS! The Natural **AKPAN** instinct is in them. **AKPAN** in position! **AKPAN** in everything! EVERYBODY IN THE WORLD **MUST ADOPT** THIS TRADITION OF **LOVE,**

PEACE, UNITY, MERCY, ONENESS, KINDNESS, TOLERANCE, EQUALITY, HONESTY and other good virtues.

THERE MUST BE **PEACE** EVERYWHERE!

Give this to MUSLIMS'!
Give this to CHRISTIANS!
Give this to JEWS!
Give to all people of all RELIGIONS!
GIVE THIS INFORMATION TO EVERYBODY IN THE WHOLE WORLD!

There should not be any evil tradition or hiding under any religion any I am this or I am that!' and cause problems for people any longer. There is no other law, or religion, or government than **LOVE YE ONE ANOTHER, PEACE, ONENESS, EQUALITY, KINDNESS WITH MY HOLY SPIRIT OF TRUTH,** because I have test all and they all have fail, Religions has failed, Governments has failed, everyone has failed, now **I THE FATHER GOD ALMIGHTY** taking control of everything in heaven and on earth.

SEND THIS INFORMATION TOGETHER WITH **MY LOVE LETTER** titled *I LOVE YOU - I LOVE YOU TOO* and *THE SUPREME FUTURE* TO THE WHOLE WORLD. SEND ALL TO THEM!

Let everybody hear this information. If they harden their heart what happened to all those who hardened their hearts against the voice of God will befall them and their blood will be upon them. That is it!

WHAT **I** HAVE GIVEN NOW IS THE NEW AND ONLY TRADITION **AKPAN** AND ALL PEOPLE OF THE WORLD MUST FOLLOW.

This is the end of Part Three.

PART FOUR
CONCLUSIONS

Yes! Today! It pleases **ME THE FATHER GOD** to give the **CONCLUSION** of this *ESIEN EMANA AKPAN 'THE AFRICAN PROBLEM'*. Therefore, this is the concluding part of this **FATHER'S TALK (GOD PRESENT)** Lecture Revelation.

INTRODUCTION: **THE REMEDY**

I have explained what caused all the problems, the downfall, the low mentality and the lack of love that resulted in darkness. You now know that when you don't have love you are in darkness. You are in a death zone.

You also understand that all the primitive behaviours right from the beginning are because **AFRICA** is the experimental ground. That was where the school started.

The school ground is like children's playground. You can see their characters as *chaka-chaka, chaka-chaka, and chaka-chaka!* They exhibit immature behaviours being that they do things anyhow, anyhow! They display underdevelopment and portray unsophisticated characteristics even till today, but **I** will correct all of them!

The corrections are not going to be physical though. It will be from the Mental Attitude of their spirits souls, from the understanding, from the idea which is from the spirit soul. It is only from today that **I THE FATHER GOD** HAS RELEASED THE NEW SPIRITS OF UNDERSTANDING, OF UNITY TO CHANGE THE **AFRICAN** LIVES IN TOTALITIES. You will see, from the next ten to fifteen to twenty-five to fifty years that **AFRICA** will be the sweet talk of the whole universe.

AFRICANS ARISE!

BE REARRANGED!

LIFT UP AND BEHAVE AS THE FATHER!

TAKE CARE OF THE WHOLE WORLD!

There will be no jealousy because other people from other parts of the world, especially the western world are fade-up with **AFRICANS** and their characters! So, they want to see a change for **AFRICA** and **AFRICANS.**

In fact, EVERYBODY WILL BE SO HAPPY TO HEAR THAT **THE FATHER GOD ALMIGHTY** HAS RELEASED THE REAL REMEDY FOR **AFRICANS,** for **AKPAN.** As well as for first wives, first daughters, first children, first in positions, first in the government, the prime minister, president, Head of State. Even for the Kings and the Queens who stand at the fence and make orders and assume that others should worship them because they do not know that they are servants.

If you want to be an important person, you should be a servant. If you want to be the senior, your position is to serve. In fact, **AKPAN** is a servant to the rest of the people just like your mother and father were the first to serve you.

AFRICANS are servants to the whole world. When you however call them servants, they are annoyed. You don't know that the servant position is an elected position, an honourable position and the position with respect. The Servants of God are Kings and Queens to the whole world. When you call them Christ Servants, certain people think they are second-class citizens. Anybody that thinks like that is a cursed person!

You want to tell **ME** now that like 'The Senior Christ Servant His Royal Majesty King Solomon David Jesse ETE is a second-class citizen of this world?

Whom would the **WORD** know first?

Whom would the **WORD** respect first?

Whom would **I THE FATHER GOD** know first? **MY Self, MY ears, MY eyes** and everything else of **ME** focus on Him. That is the reason if you bring your trouble around Him you are in trouble.

Don't you see as those who work under the capacity of **THE WORD** if you bring trouble to them you are in trouble! Anywhere they go they are, one hundred percent secure! Have you heard that?

From today, if you are a Servant of God, do NOT fear! You might feel bad that people call you a servant. You shouldn't. An **AFRICAN** is a Servant and Servant means **Father.** You serve your children and in turn, your children will serve you.

What happens in the nature of a father? You have children with your wife. When they were babies, you probably cleaned their bottoms and provided for them and when they grow up, they in turn will take care of you. They would do the same thing you did for them for you. That is **OOO**. Life is going around, around and around.

When a child reaches the age of eighteen, even sixteen they are no more under their parents, so they are free.

A father can never be free. A mother can never be free. So, you can see that naturally the **solid-skin** humans, the **dark-skin**, the **AFRICANS** are the fathers and mothers of all human beings. They can trace their origin. Can you trace your origin? The whole of **AFRICANS** and the **West Indies** can trace where they came from because they have link to their origin in Africa. They have root. So, do not destroy that root **AFRICANS.**

LOVE IS THE ROOT OF AFRICA. And also is **unity, peace, righteousness, mercy, kindness** and **THE HOLY SPIRIT.**

Do not go to bring witchcraft to destroy **AFRICA.**

Do not go to bring talisman and all sorts of bad things from India or from anywhere else to destroy **AFRICA.** No wicked evil things are originally from **AFRICA**. **I** can tell you how all those evil things came to **AFRICA**. Thereafter **AFRICANS** started to believe in talisman.

The first witchcraft came to **EGYPT** when Satan established his temple in Egypt to fight against the ruler ship of **THE FATHER GOD. I** marked out Egypt to be the First Centre, but things had to take a different turn when Satan came to Egypt, because of the spirit soul of Cain the original Vampire. **I** will tell you a small secret today. When **I** created Adam and Lucifer deceived Adam and Eve, **I** sent them away from the Garden of Eden, because of what happened. Lucifer went to where they went to establish and nursed them. (**I AM** cutting short the story. **I** won't tell you everything at this point).

When Adam came back as Christ, the same spirit outside the gate wanted to kill Christ so **I** had to send Christ and his parents back to **AFRICA.** Do you know the meaning of that? The reason was that Egypt was where there was security. That is also, where the Egyptian mummy is.

Egyptian mummy (THE CARE TAKER OF WEALTH THE CALLED **"MMA-MMONG" GOD IN CHARGE OF WATER** (THE BASEMENT WORLD) where the true nature of a fair or soft and lighter skin human being came from as **I** revealed to you- well you don't know the whole story as at yet, but there is a message on that. Egyptian mummy is the actual born physical evil that the spirit Jezebel was using to conjure evil as magic to destroy the Temple of God in **AFRICA.** That was Cain at work, the Lucifer in incarnation.

Anybody that goes to carry the Egyptian mummy and all those things from India and from China are doing the work of evil. You see them in Egypt. You see them in India. You see them in China. They all live in dragon and serpent and are from mammy water. They are all water problems.

The civilization of earth also has link to that. Anyway, that is not what we are talking today.

The good and evil work together but the good supersedes evil and takes ruler ship. THE PERFECT CIVILIZATION OF THIS WORLD IS FROM 'LOVE ONE ANOTHER.'

When they started to conjure the evil god, they called it witchcraft. That is the spirit they use for magic and for all sorts of things. They use that to command things. And they use the seven Books of Moses to do the conjuring. They are all Spoken Words. But NOW **I** WITHDRAW THE POTENCY FROM ALL NEGATIVE WORDS! None of those things is going to work again. **I** HAVE RENDERED THEM USELESS AND EMPTY! **I** have now replaced these words with positive words. It is the Tree of Life and birth to override the Tree of Death. These are positive pronouncements taking charge now in the whole world. In that light, what you have to do is for you to believe this remedy.

The remedy that **I AM** revealing today is that everything you see on this earth has turned around for good. And the situations of **AFRICA, AKPAN** and everybody else should be based on **Love One Another** and **unity** and **peace.** That is when everything will be good. That is the starting for the remedy. It is **love, love, love, unity** and **peace** for everybody. You must **serve as a father and not as a slave.**

Everybody on earth should respect the senior person. Give the respect that is from **THE FATHER GOD. Love the brotherhood. Fear God. Honour the King.**

A: **SECOND THOUGHT IS THE REMEDY FOR ALL AKPAN PROBLEMS**

This is **the time for Second Thought for all human beings.** All **AFRICANS,** all Heads of organizations, countries, states and communities, all **AKPAN,** all **ADIAGHA** and as matter of fact everybody, this is the chance given for your Second Thought.

Do not say 'I am too big for this or I am going to this church, I am of this religion or that religion and so I can't read this thing.' Do not give any excuses to avoid having this information. For **I** know that one person will read and give to another person. Another person will read and pass the information to yet another person and so on. Then the news of the **REMEDY** for all **AFRICA'S** and problems of all **AKPANS'** problems will spread all over the world. The root of all the problems will now be solved through THE SPOKEN WORD, THE PANACEA.

I, THE WORD, THE FIRST, IS THE ONLY ONE THAT CAN SOLVE THE PROBLEMS THAT PLAGUE THE FIRST. I HAVE SOLVED THE PROBLEM TODAY!

Therefore, PASS THIS INFORMATION TO EVERY HUMAN BEING ON EARTH so that everybody will be happy because when the FIRST MAN in the family is happy everybody is happy.

If the first person is good everybody is good. If the first person is bad the rest of the people term to be bad because this person would want everybody to be bad, he would want everybody to be wicked if he is wicked. He would want everybody to be traditional person if the first man is into tradition. If you do not want to join, the first person to do rubbish the person will hate you. That is why the wicked people don't like those who declare the truth. Nonetheless, all the FIRSTS MUST DECLARE THE TRUTH ABOUT **THE TRUTH** today!

B: **THIS IS THE END PROBLEMS FOR AFRICAN NATIONS**

Alleluia! *Alleluia!*
Alleluia! *Alleluia!*

Alleluia! *Alleluia!*
**ENYE! ODUDU! ABASI MI! OOO! ZIM, ZIM, ZIM! ASSASSU!
Positive! Positive! Positive!**
Today is the end for all **AFRICAN** problems, all **AKPANS'** problems, all senior people's problems, all those in senior posts and positions' problems! **I, THE SUPREME WORD, THE SPOKEN WORD** HAVE USED THIS **SUPREME WORD SEASON** to eradicate all jealousy, all envy, all tribalism and all the things that bring woes and problems in the whole world all those problems. And **I** infuse the correct instinct, the correct emotions, the correct feelings, the correct understanding of making pronouncements of positive words for all senior citizens of this earth, the senior persons, those in positions of authority so that things will work well with them and for them, in the name of Our Lord Jesus Christ. Amen!

If you believe this Lecture Revelation, kneel down, make

pronouncements and confess the wrong beliefs you had and all the wrongs you have been doing. It does not matter even if you were into the mummy spirit soul of Egypt, even the serpent spirit soul of India, even the dragon spirit soul of China, from that to the pouring of libation in Africa and the scientist beliefs of the western world and all other things that destroy the world. All these negative spirit-souls that destroy the world including pomposity, arrogance, cunning, strife, misplaced loyalty and all the rest of the ills of the world are all subject to The Truth Spirit. When you confess and apologise **I, THE SUPREME WORD** will bring **The Truth Spirit** into you, which will include, **love, peace, mercy, kindness, joy, honesty, unity, equality, oneness and I** mean the genuine ones.

Not the one that people say they are practicing equality, but are crafty. Their activities in that regard are cunning. They reek of craftiness and deceit. Not the ones people say they are doing charity but hire or acquire weapons to kill people instead. Those are not the behaviours **I** mean.

I mean the proper Red Cross work; the proper human life savers, like the American Red Cross, the Europeans Red Cross. For all the people that go about saving lives **I** have given them the Holy Spirit to continue to do the positive works. As well as the **AFRICANS** and indeed everybody in the world **I** have given them The HOLY SPIRIT. Joy! Joy! Joy on earth, in the name of Our Lord Jesus Christ, Amen!

THIS IS THE END PROBLEM FOR ALL PROBLEMS THROUGH **THE PANACEA,** THE PRONOUNCEMENT.
THE WORD OF GOD has entered into the world today. In the light of that, speak what is good. Think well, speak well, see well, hear well and do well and all is well with you and your family, in the name of Our Lord Jesus Christ, Amen!

C: YOU MUST BE SUBJECTED TO THE TRUTH LIFE OF THE FATHER GOD

Since everything now is new, you should celebrate **THE SUPREME WORD OF THE UNIVERSE.** Share what you have with love with one another. Subject yourself to the Holy Spirit of love and be truthful. Promote this WORD! Promote this INFORMATION! Love One Another.

Do not reject **The Truth! It not be** because of your church, your cult, your country or because you are **dark-skin** or **solid-skin** African, or **light-skin** or **soft-skin** European and from other western worlds and other humans' skin colours in-between that you should reject this **Truth**. Do not reject this **TRUTH** because of being educated, because of being a man or a woman and because of any reason at all. Accept this **TRUTH** because of oneness of **THE FATHER GOD'S**

NATURE and oneness of LOVE is the HOLY SPIRIT OF TRUTH.

As you promote this information, as you promote good things then **I THE FATHER GOD** will promote you. I know those who promote good things and Good things will promote you by themselves. Then you will see that your environment will be a good environment.

Through you, your family will be well.

Through you, all your things will be well.

Through you, your life will progress.

Through you, the whole world will be in peace.

Through you, Muslims and Christian will be in peace. Through you, **Truth** will always triumph.

Do not be afraid to tell the truth. Always declare the truth. Unite the whole world with this truth information and everybody will be fine!

If you occupy any office for instance as a president, a king, a queen, a head of the church, head of any organization or department; a worker, a civil servant or ordinary servant or anything else you are to use this information as a remedy for the entire world. If you are father, a mother, a child, a senior sister as **AKPAN, Udoh, Adiagha** and anything at all, you are to use this information as a remedy for the entire world. And **I THE FATHER GOD** will bless you and elevate your soul, in the name of Our Lord Jesus Christ. Amen!

D: **YOU MUST NOT WORSHIP ANY IDOL**

This is very, very serious! If you still believe in talisman, concoctions, invocation, secret books of any negative means; call angels, believe in any infidels; go to the trees to worship or go to the forest or water for any negative activities; you still pour libation in the way of worship, then **MY** attention is not with you. **MY SPIRIT** is not with you! And **I** will not take it kindly with you! **I** will not support you. **I** will not sanction anything for you. You will see hell!

However, if from today you throw away your talisman, you throw away all those secret books, you resign from all the secret cults where you are a member; you do not do any wickedness, you do not join any bad or evil gang then **MY** Spirit will be with you. Just forget about that vow you took in that wicked cult or secret society. Make a vow with the Holy Spirit from today and all is well with you.

All the people that have entered cults and vowed to the cult, come and vow to **THE SUPREME WORD.** Join HRM King Solomon David Jesse **ETE** to celebrate **THE SUPREME WORD** and vow therein. Even though the other vow you made in that cult was the WORD, **I THE SUPREME WORD** does not know that one. Vow again here to **THE SUPREME WORD.** Promote this WORD! Promote this information! And **I WILL SEAL YOU WITH THE SEAL OF SALVATION THAT THOSE CULTS WILL NOT HAVE POWER OVER YOU! DEMONS WILL NOT HAVE POWER OVER YOU! NOTHING WILL HAVE POWER OVER YOU! I WILL SEAL YOU WITH THE SEAL OF SALVATION, THE SEAL OF THE HOLY SPIRIT! I THE SUPREME WORD OF THE UNIVERSE WILL BE THE MARK OF SALVATION ON YOU!**

HOWEVER, if you deviate and would not support the truth then you will perish. Nevertheless, if you accept the Truth, The Truth will set you free from any form of slavery, any form of captivity, in the name and blood of Our Lord Jesus Christ, Amen!

So, you must not worship any idol of any form when you sign up for **THE SUPREME FATHER GOD ALMIGHTY,** when you sign up for the

TRUTH. As for **AFRICA, THE FATHER AND MOTHER LAND, THE MILKY LAND**, if you want to enjoy that place, starting from Nigeria, Ghana and all the countries of Africa and everywhere in Africa, do not worship idols. Even in Egypt, you are going to see what will happen in Egypt. Egypt is the centre, the Throne of **THE FATHER GOD.** That was where Christ was and that is why **I** put down **MY** feet. That was where **I** took salvation to humankind.

FROM TODAY! **I** HAVE REDEEMED EGYPT FOR **THE FATHER GOD! I** HAVE RETURNED THE FIRST GLORY THAT WAS EGYPT, THE FIRST CIVILIZATION OF **THE HOLY SPIRIT** TO EGYPT!

You will see what will happen in Egypt, the good things, that is. Egypt is at the Northern most part of Africa the boundary between Africa and the earth. And from Today! **I** have joined Egypt with Nigeria! **I** have joined Egypt with Ghana! **I** have joined them with all other African countries! **I** have joined the United Kingdom, America North and South, all Europe, all Asia and **AFRICA** together!

I HAVE PUT EVERYWHERE IN THE WORLD TOGETHER AND THEY BECOME ONE!

One world!

One unity!

One agreement of no more WAR on earth!

One **SUPREME CELEBRATION,** which is **THE SUPREME WORD CELEBRATION, THE HOLY SPIRIT OF TRUTH, THE IKOT! THE ABASI! THE AMEN!** That is the link through which everyone in the world shall see peace and joy.

No more worshipping of dragon!

No more worshipping of Egyptian mummy!

No more worshipping of serpents or snakes!

No more worshipping of idols and those other things!

ONE **GOD, THE FATHER GOD** SURPASSES ALL THINGS. LOVE ONE

ANOTHER! That is the order of the day. Now and forever to **THE SUPREME FUTURE!**

E: **YOU MUST HUMBLE YOURSELF IN YOUR FATHER'S HOUSE AFRICANS**

All **AFRICANS** are in their **FATHER'S** House. That is **THE FATHER GOD'S** premises, **THE SUPREME PREMISES OF THE FATHER GOD, THE CREATOR.**
THE WHOLE WORLD IS THE SUPREME PREMISES OF **THE FATHER GOD.** Everywhere you are, you are before **THE FATHER GOD,** GOD PRESENT so you must humble yourself. Anything you do, remember that you have **THE FATHER GOD.** Since you now have the awareness that this is the condition then all is well. That is all **I** want from humankind.

Everything you do from now must be all about **THE FATHER GOD! THE**

FATHER GOD! THE FATHER GOD! You are all children of **THE FATHER GOD.** We are all Servants of **THE FATHER GOD.**

Solomon said, "Father don't take me as a son, take me as a servant. I am not worthy to be your son". And that is why he is a prodigal son. Every human being who has sinned is a prodigal son and a prodigal daughter, but when you repent and serve your **FATHER GOD** by loving one another then that is all! If you happen to think you are righteous, then you are pompous.

You believe that the position of **AKPAN** of **AFRICA** is your merit. What made you think that you merit anything in this world as a sinner?

Do you practice love?
Are you holy?
You fornicate!
You commit adultery.
You commit abortion!

You do all sorts of bad things. What made you think you merit the position you hold, if not the love of **THE FATHER GOD?** So, if you know that it is through love that you are there, use love to treat other people. Do not use arrogance because nobody merits anything in this world. Everybody is a prodigal son. Love One Another is the only remedy. When you do that then, you have humbled yourself before **THE FATHER GOD.**

F: **AKPAN THE FIRSTBORN IN THE WORLD SHOULD LOVE**

That is the instruction. **AFRICA** the FIRST SON, the first brother, the first sister, the senior in the family, the first in position, the head of any country of the world, the head of government, President, the King, Prime Minister, and any other post you have as a senior post you must love and serve one another with humility. All the people under you are your children. You are representing **THE FATHER GOD.**

Every self is representing **THE FATHER GOD, THE SPOKEN WORD.**

If you mistreat them, you are debased! This is an Ordinance and an Order! Whether you believe it or not, so, think about it from today.

G: **AKPAN MUST JOIN IN THE CELEBRATION OF THE UNIVERSAL SUPREME WORD SEASON CELEBRATION**

As **I** said before the remedy for all **AKPAN** is to join in *THE UNIVERSAL SUPREME WORD SEASON CELEBRATION.* Ask to know the meaning of it and what to do.

There is no special thing to do. You can speak and you can think. You know the meaning of the Spoken Word. The Spoken Word you have in you is in your heart but **THE SUPREME WORD OF THE UNIVERSE** engineers you to speak.

The Life, the CREATOR, **THE FATHER GOD, THE SPIRIT. HE IS THE MAKER. HE IS THE SUPREME WORD OF THE UNIVERSE.**

If you refuse this that means you do not believe this information and you don't believe, it is the truth and that means that **I** can call you to **MYSELF** at anytime.

With this information a lot people could die. Something will happen because **I** will NOT take it kindly with anybody that fights against this Ordinance and anyone that refuses to believe The TRUTH.

If you refuse this, you refuse the **WORD** and you are not entitled again to speak or to sing. But if you surrender with humility, and are sober with faith and joy then, you are going to see the glory of God in you no matter who you are. Even if you have one hundred heads, The **WORD** is your **CREATOR** so you must obey this **WORD**!

If you fight against this idea, you are not fighting anybody, but you fight against **ME THE WORD** and **I** know how to treat you.

THE SUPREME CELEBRATION ON EARTH is *THE UNIVERSAL SUPREME WORD SEASON CELEBRATION* that covers all aspects of things. Celebrate it! You are the celebrant. Anything at all that is positive you can do, do during the ten-day period of the celebration, which is from First of October to the Tenth of October of every year by the old system calendar, (presently used). However, in the new calendar it is the seventh month – From the First of the Seventh month to the Tenth of that Seventh month. You should celebrate with the highest magnitude as a Mark of Honour for **THE FATHER GOD, THE SUPREME WORD** and then you will see how **I** will promote you.

Celebrate in your church, your religion and your government. Celebrate wherever you are and in whatever relationship you are. However, bear in mind that celebrating **THE SUPREME WORD** has nothing to do with religion. It has nothing to do with churches or any other place of worship. Rather, it has everything to do with the LIVES of all human beings. Cooperate with one another. **I AM** using this to test and see the human beings that are positive. Unite the whole world and be one world, one WORD and one LIFE, now and forever. That is **MY** ORDER!

H: **ALL AKPAN TO TAKE EVOLUTION AWAY FROM NEGATIVE NATURE OF CAIN LUCIFER REPRESENTATIVE ON EARTH**

Take evolution away from Cain. Take evolution away from Lucifer. You know about Lucifer. She goes about causing all sorts of problems between husband and wife, between church members, between family members, between nations as well as between neighbours.

She is the one that causes all the problems, the fighting and killing till now because she is jealous. She has nowhere to live. She goes about looking for victims. All accidents, all bloodshed, all cults are from Lucifer. She established all sorts of traditions, all sorts of cults and the killing of people and all sorts of other evil things, which you all know about and join. You should take evolution away from it.

It is better that you died because of denying Satan than you live and accept Satan, because it is not going to be well with you when you do that. Those who save their lives will lose it. But if you follow this TRUTH and save the TRUTH instead of saving your life then, **I THE FATHER GOD** will save your life.

I: **THEN I THE SUPREME WORD OF THE UNIVERSE WILL DO WHAT?**

I will rescue your life.
I will save you.
I will register your name in the Book of Life, in the Book of the WORD.

The WORD can never die.

The WORD lives for eternity.

Go to heaven and come back the WORD is OOO, Spirit, Soul and Physical. The WORD goes round and round and comes back.

The WORD is your ancestor.

The WORD is **THE FATHER GOD.**

The WORD is everything.

So put your faith in **ME.** Trust **THE FATHER GOD.** When you put your faith in **ME** and listen to the WORD and accept the WORD and acknowledge the WORD, then you stop talking negatively. Do not allow any negative word to come out from your mouth about this word and in your general life.

Don't wish anybody any negativism, because **I** have ordered that from now onwards what you say follows you. If you sit down and wish somebody anything good, that goodness will come to you first before it goes to that person. Everybody should have the mouth to speak for him or herself. You don't need to *borrow-borrow* words.

You don't need anybody to bless you. If you want something, talk to **THE FATHER GOD** and **THE FATHER GOD** will bless you. This is not the time of primitive ideas. 'I am going to a big person to bless me. I am going to the tree to bless me.' **THE FATHER GOD** blesses you directly. What you wish yourself and wish others is that which blesses you. When you do good things, the good things know how to bless you. Everything you sow you shall reap no matter what it is and who you are.

If you would do evil, kill and you do all sorts of bad things and a priest or a preacher that does not know what your are doing will bless you and say GOD bless you, do think **I** will bless you? No! **I** will rather bless that preacher. You went and killed and afterwards brought twenty million to the preacher. The preacher says, 'oh I have seen a man of God I will bless him.' Just like Abraham that went and killed people. Do you think Abraham was blessed?

What was the blessing of Abraham? I only blessed Abraham later when he realized he was not supposed to kill and he was not supposed to steal. Then he surrendered all that to **THE FATHER GOD** and denied them. Don't you see what happened to Abraham? Wandering!

Do you think it is good to kill and have blood in your hands? You shed innocent blood. You destroy people and you think you are blessed? Remember, nobody lords it over anybody anymore.

EVERYBODY IS LIBERATED AND IS FREE IN THE WHOLE UNIVERSE, through the name and the blood of Our Lord Jesus Christ. Amen

You must respect your seniors. You must respect anybody that is in a big position. You must love. That is reciprocal. Then **I the WORD, the SUPREME WORD OF THE**

UNIVERSE will bless you. **I** know how to bless you according to your deeds.

AO: THE LECTURE REVELATION IS THE REMEDY FOR ALL PROBLEMS IN AFRICA, AKPAN AND EVERYBODY IN THE WHOLE UNIVERSE

Use this Lecture Revelation as "Manual of Life Elevation", "Manual Of Improvement", "Manual Of Rearrangement Of Life", Manual that all **AKPAN** and all **Adiagha** as those in any first positions and everybody else should use to guide themselves, even if you are spirit that turned to become human being use this information to help your soul.

Forget about who you are and what you are. It does not matter. This WORD is final. You are not bigger than the WORD that made you to be alive and since you are alive, it is the life that is bigger than you are that

lives life in you. So, the LIFE has instructed you. That is what you should be doing.
Get **MANUAL OF LIFE**.
Get **LIFE EXTENSION MANUAL**
Get **MANUAL OF THE SPOKEN WORD**
Get **MANUAL OF INVESTMENT WITH GOD.**
Everything you want to hear about **THE FATHER'S TALK (GOD PRESENT)** you will have them.

Advisably, open **THE FATHER'S TALK (GOD PRESENT)** Library in your family because this is ARCHIVE RECORDS so that you acquaint yourself with the instructions of **THE FATHER GOD** before it is too late.
LET **MY** PEACE AND BLESSING ABIDE WITH THE ENTIRE WORLD, NOW AND FOREVER MORE, AMEN!
ENYE! ODUDU! ABASI MI! OOO! ZIM, ZIM, ZIM! ASSASSU! POSITIVE! POSITIVE! POSITIVE!
This is the pronouncement for **THE UNIVERSAL SUPREME WORD**

SEASON CELEBRATION that was from the First of October to the Tenth of October, but extended to the Twelfth of October for the Thanksgiving Service.

I THE SUPREME LOVE, THE FATHER GOD ALMIGHTY, THE SUPREME WORD OF THE UNIVERSE, THE LIGHT OF LIFE IN ALL HUMAN BEINGS, bless all human beings on earth, bless all human beings that have love, that have peace, that have joy, that have oneness, that have equality. **I** secure them. No evil will befall them. No bad things will befall them.

You will not have any problems when you deny all evils and all negative things. Forgive one another. Think well, speak well, hear well, see well and do well. Aim to support good things and deny bad things. Be truthful with all undertakings. Be truthful with everybody. Have respect for everybody and love **THE FATHER GOD.** Say to **ME, 'I Love YOU too.'**

Make sure you have that Lecture Revelation. **I AM** referring to **THE SUPREME LOVE LETTER I SENT TO THE WHOLE WORLD.**

LET MY PEACE AND BLESSING ABIDE WITH YOU! ALL IS WELL!

I BLESS ETE ROYAL UNIVERSAL FAMILY!

I BLESS HRM KING SOLOMON DAVID JESSE ETE! **I** BLESS EVERYBODY THAT CONTRIBUTES TO THIS! **I** BLESS EVERYBODY THAT BELIEVES!

Till tomorrow all **AFRICANS,** all **AKPAN** all **ADIAGHA** and every head of everywhere are blessed by The WORD when you listen to this Lecture Revelation or read and believe it, all is well with you and the entire world.

All those who celebrate **THE SUPREME WORD OF THE UNIVERSE,** recognize **THE FATHER GOD** via the **WORD,** know that The **WORD IS THE CREATOR,** and that everybody manages things through The WORD including the wife, the husband, the children, the president, the king, the manager, the teacher,…name it, are blessed by **The WORD**. Therefore, when you celebrate **The WORD** then, **I** celebrate you.

ALL IS WELL WITH THE ENTIRE WORLD, NOW AND FOREVER MORE. AMEN.

THANK YOU FATHER!

Chapter Three

"A"

THE FIRST OF ALL (AKPAN ABASI) (A of A to Z – ZAKROLLS OF ALL THINGS)

FATHER'S TALK
(GOD PRESENT)

CHRIST AI/OC/BOOE
(Saturday, Nineteenth March Two Thousand and Five)

In the Name of Our Lord Jesus Christ, In the Blood of Our Lord Jesus Christ, Now and forever more

"A"

THE FIRST OF ALL

(AKPAN ABASI)

(A of A to Z – ZAKROLLS OF ALL THINGS)

INTRODUCTION OF **A – Z**

Today, **I THE FATHER GOD** wants to decode and reveal 'The letters **A of A to Z**. Letter A, B, C to Z are Alpha and Omega. That is the Compound

FATHER GOD. Each of the letters is **GOD**, but put them together **A – Z** and it becomes **THE COMPOUND FATHER GOD**. The Lecture Revelation of today is wonderful, because that is how **I** see it, but **I** don't know how you are personally seeing it.

If you take one letter away from **A to Z,** you are in trouble. Do you understand? One letter should not be missed from **A to Z. I** formulated them. The actual civilization between the carnal man and the Spiritual human God is the alphabets. **A to Z** means **ALL** and **ALL**. In the physical reality, **A to Z** refers to The Father. So there will be a Lecture Revelation called **A to Z of THE FATHER GOD THE CREATOR OF THE UNIVERSE."** Yes! There is no space for anything negative to survive. ***I AM THE A TO Z.*** You see that! **I** do not want to talk and talk and there is no reproduction. If not so, nothing has happened yet. Don't you see that the Lecture

Revelations we are refreshing on now are the keys. You cannot come to these recent ones without passing through "**The Astrots and Innerstrots**", "**Amfar-one**", "**One = God Presence.**" "FATHER is **A to Z** and that is how **THE FATHER'S TALK** (**GOD PRESENT**) is going to link. It will link from **A to Z**. Do you think that Seventy-two million **FATHER'S TALK**, is it a small thing? So do not let **ME** 'quat' (squat). Anything you do with letters blow it and enlarge it like a mountain. Do you know what writing the Alphabets **A** to **Z** to cover a whole sheet of A4 paper is? Do you know what a mountain looks like? That is letter **A**, if you want to write, first, let **ME** show you, *demonstrates by writing the alphabet A to cover the sheet of a paper.* You should make the letters big, big, and even bigger than A1 side of paper, extending it sideways. Do you see how this baby Semsem makes his hands? Do you know the meaning of that? It means the whole world, the two hands, not one. It is like that. It stands for the four corners of the world. This time, **I** do not want to be 'quatting' (squatting) Semsem says. Come now **I AM** ready for you. **I** want proper students; **I** want proper students, students of the Higher Self. You know that you people have to go home and establish this school. When you would do that, you will set one up in Biakpan. You will go to many places to establish this school without King Solomon David Jesse ETE being there. You will just carry all these Lectures Revelations here, to go and educate people through giving them. As soon as you start to give the lecture, **I** will give the inspiration and **I** will connect them. Do you know Ikot Okwo where the school started physically? There will be many students there studying full time. The certificate **I** will give them is the certificate of Brotherhood Mastership. That is the certificate people will use for employment in the new world." This will be for everything! Like being a Social

Worker! How do you socialize when you do not understand **THE FATHER GOD**?

Do you think they will use all these present mundane certificates to work? The required certificate in the future new world would be the Certificate of practising **LOVE FOR ONE ANOTHER**; having **PATIENCE** and **UNDERSTANDING** with one another will teach you how to deal with human beings and that is the **A to Z Certificate**. All these lessons will be assigned numbers. Have you started listing them? Mfon have you started listing them? *"Yes Father but not alphabetically."* No, **I AM** not talking about alphabetical listing; it is not what **I** mean. There will be Lectures Revelations that represent **A** of the Alphabets and cover **A –Z**. The Lecture Revelation will start called "**A**"; another will follow called "**B**" and will cover all the letters of the Alphabet. **I** will reveal what they each stand for in **MY** components. Do you know that? Where is the Lecture Revelation, titled '*THE DESIGNER*'? Is it there? *"Yes Father."* Bring it I want to show you something in it. Okay if you can't find it leave it for now. All of them will come. All of them will come out one by one wherever they are. All alphabets represent one of **THE FATHER GOD'S** components.

You know that I created everything, therefore I know what I put in people, and I know what I will use people to do. Whatsoever nature Ephraim is, I will carry out **AMIENTICE –SURTIERS** on him. Write it out in bold with a dash between the word. "**AMIENTICE -** what? Asked The *Father, interrupting Disem's reading. Father corrected as written above., then added albeit jokingly*, I thought you pronounced it 'Ashanti.' *(We all laughed)* **AMIENTICE – SURTIERS** means to 'sort you out'!

Have you started listing these words? I said you should compile all these **FATHER'S TALK** words you come across. If you gather one hundred to one thousand words of them, then you have started a new spiritual language. **I** do not mean Biakpan. Yes! Stop there so far.

Yes, that is the key, the key for **A to Z**. That was what **I** was looking for in the '**CHANGEOVER**' Lecture Revelation.

Part B
*Introduction of **A – Z***
"THE THEORY OF EVERYTHING"

THE THEORY OF EVERYTHING, HE IS THE FATHER, the INVISIBLE and VISIBLE control centre where HE and SHE are in vibration known as **MATUM – (The Vibrator),** the super natural boiler producing cold and heat, each on AB (twelve) capacities. That is where nature gets its shape manifestation in the form of strings of

O's.

ooOOOOOOOOOOOOOOOOOOOO

It is endlessness, endless phenomenon, which forms the Super Natural bubbles. The transformation into shapes is the stimulation of **THE FATHER** and **THE MOTHER GOD'S** energy generated as the water and the air, which is the wave of life, the nature of all things Brotherhood, the String of Nature and the energy of creation as **THE STRING OF LIFE**.

Yes! Today's Lecture Revelation is very, a-very important. It is one of the greatest revelations that **I, THE FATHER GOD** has decided to give to benefit humankind for generations upon generations. It has been the case that in the history of humankind, human beings have decided to take the glory they are supposed to give to **ME THE FATHER GOD THE CREATOR OF THE UNIVERSE** for themselves. All humans can only share the glory with **THE FATHER**

GOD, but man should not usurp the glory of **THE FATHER GOD,** because a human being is an empty vessel and cannot exist without **ME THE FATHER GOD.** As you all know, **I THE FATHER GOD, I AM THE EXISTENCE MYSELF. I AM** the Genesis of all creations and MY SON, THE SUPREME WORD is the potency of **MY** Soul, and He is the Generator, the 'Converting Machine' that brings everything from the spirit to the physical reality. In view of that, The **WORD**, the phrase 'The **WORD**, The Zeal, The Stamp, The Manifest, The Maker, compounded **HIMSELF** in the component called **A – Z** and that is **THE FATHER'S MANY SELVES.**

ZAKROLLS (ZERO) DOES NOT MEAN EMPTINESS

A to Z is **I THE FATHER GOD MYSELF**. It is the compound **GOD, THE FATHER.** You can call it spirit, soul or physical manifestation. **A to Z** incorporates into one entity which is

THE UNIVERSAL SUPREME WORD. When you read the book '**HE IS THE WORD**', then you will know that there is nothing **THE FATHER GOD** would do to manifest in the physical reality without '**THE WORD**' and '**THE WORD** constitutes **MY** energy of **A to Z** letters. **A to Z** is interwoven or incorporated in the word **Alpha** and **Omega**. So letter 'A' stands for **Alpha - *Akpan*. *Akpan*** - means the first-born son. ***Akpa*** -means the first of everything **AFRICA**.

First – **Akpan**, the first born; First – **Akpa** and **A** as **Abasi**. Anything constituted by **A** refers to **Alpha** and **Z** refers to **Omega, THE CONCLUSION**, and that is the First and the Last. Alpha, -A links to what is called **O – Circle**. Circle Ring means '**IKARA**', which is **O – Olumba**. So in **A** to **Z**, **A** means **Alpha- ash NTONGO**– Adam and Circle Ring, which is **O,** means **Omega- dust – OBU**. **O** is the circle ring as the protection, which incorporate **A to Z**. It is everything created, not created and that will be created including everything that will exist, that exist and has existed. Everything incorporates into A **to Z**. When you start something, it means it is not yet complete, but when you end something then it means that it is completed. It is from **A** to **Z which means** from **Alpha** to **Omega** – **A** and **O**.

People erroneously believe that when they call something zero, it means nothingness. Today **I AM** going to reveal the meaning of zero. Zero does not mean nothingness. Zero does not mean zero literally. It is not, nought, which is nothingness; this **Zero is O** - that is a circle, which occupies an endless space. How can you refer to something that occupies space to be empty? Circle means **INCLUDED**. Another day **I** will reveal **Circle** as **Included**. And that is how **I, THE FATHER GOD** is Included. When you draw a circle, you have covered a space, which is the **Zero** as **ZAKROLL**, the completion.

ZAKROLL – means **Exactly Completed in Components as a Circle** – **ZAKROLLS**.

ZAKROLLS spelt – Z-A-K and then R-O-L-L-S as in rolling. **ZAKROLLS** means **Completed Circle** and the cycle of completion as components that are actually completed and are a completed component and a complete phenomenon. The phenomenon called **INCLUDED** is **ME THE FATHER GOD** as **THE COMPLETION.** Complete! **A to Z** means complete! The pronunciation of **ZAKROLL** from the slip of tongue resulted in zero. It is a missed actual pronunciation of **ZAKROLL** that coined zero or circle. All these pronunciations are as a result of the tongue that twists. It is **THE FATHER GOD** who has formulated **HIMSELF** into these components of **THE SUPREME WORD**. Allelu-u-u! *"Alleluia!"*

Enye! Odudu! Abasi mi! OOO! Zim, Zim, Zim! Assassu!

I want all the inhabitants of the universe, all creations especially humankind to be serious about this Lecture Revelation. But of course, humankind comes in many divided categories. They consist of the four living creatures. Out of the four groups the three categories, are animal, bird and fish and they will doubt or joke about these things, but one of the categories will be serious with all the **FATHER'S TALK GOD PRESENT** Lectures Revelations. The one that will be serious is **AKPAN - AKPAN** ETE that is **First** of **ALL**. ETE means **ALL**. **FATHER** means **ALL** as everything. First is, **THE FIRST OF ALL**, which is **AKPAN ABASI** (FIRST GOD) and **AKPAN ETE (FIRST FATHER)**. Do you see that **I** have brought **The First of ALL as MY FIRST SON** back into the world? The **First Son of God** means **THE SUPREME WORD.** It is the first building that housed **THE UNIVERSAL SUPREME WORD** and it started with letter **A**, which means **Alpha** - Adam. In effect, **ADAM** is the First of All, then **OBU – Omega** is the completion of all, therefore when you see Alpha and Omega, it means that the **FIRST SON THE PERSONIFIED WORD** and **HIS FATHER THE PERSONIFIED HOLY SPIRIT OF TRUTH** with all HIS CREATIONS BROTHERHOOD are here.

People say that there is no secret. Who says there is no secret? There's the secret of **THE FATHER GOD**, the secret of the Son, the secret of the Holy Spirit and the secret of creation and all are buried under **A to Z. A – AFRICA – AKPAN. A – Abasi** is the **FIRST-BORN** creation, which is **Adam as Alpha.** That is first HOUSE - MAN. The last is **Omega,** which is **Olumba Obu** (SPIRIT AND DUST) and that is **THE FATHER GOD, THE CREATOR OF THE UNIVERSE**. It means **ALL as** the **First** of **All**.

Anytime you say first of all things, it means **AKPAN IKO (ABASI) – AKPAN ETE, AFRICA, THE FIRST WORD, THE FIRST MAN,** and **THE FIRST LAND. THE FATHER GOD** in another Supreme understanding language is called **ALL, ALL IS FATHER, ALL** and **ALL IS THE FATHER AND THE SON. ALL** and **ALL** means **ALL** in the spirit, and in the soul, and then **ALL** and **ALL** live in the physical truth, the human personified **GOD (OLUMBA OLUMBA OBU). ALL** and **ALL** means **Alpha** and **Omega**. It means **ALL** and **ALL**; the **FIRST** and the **LAST**; **THE FATHER** and **THE SON;** the **BEGINNING** and the **ENDING-LESS.** In the beginning, **HE IS THE SPIRIT** manifested to be a human being. The endless is the spirit going back to the soul and all of them form **Alpha** and **Omega** – **A** to **Z**. So in between **A** to **Z** are B, C, D, etcetera, etcetera, but for today this is **A of A to Z** Lecture Revelation.

From the year two thousand and one, you must incorporate anything you do into **A TO Z.** That is the new life that everyone would be living in the new world of **THE FATHER GOD'S SUPREME FUTURE**. **I** have coded every human being in one of the letters. Each of the letters formulates the **STAR** of the human nature which individual personified **WORD** takes to come and into the world by birth. You are assigned a **NAME** as a manifestation of one of THE SUPREME WORD components of **THE FATHER GOD**, which is one of the letters from **A TO Z.** You bear it as a sign with which you are known with in the spirit soul. **I** can say ***A DASH A PLUS A MINUS A*** is equal to **ADAM** - AFRICA - ALPHA (A_A+A-A= ***ADAM***). That is how **I** decode every human being, and that is how **I** make people and give them their **STAR OF NATURE** and what they have to do in the physical life. The code of your star is in your forehead and it appears in your palm, which is

MY spiritual computer monitor screen as the inbuilt projector of human self. Every human's left hand is his or her output spiritual computer screen and the right hand is his or her input in the spiritual computer screen which is your heart, which is your spirit and that is the hard disk where everything installs and that is **I** THE **FATHER GOD *OPERATING IN EVERY HUMAN BEING SPIRITUALLY***. The Spirit that you took to came to this world is **MY BUBBLE** and that is referred to as **'THE THEORY OF EVERYTHING' THE BUBBLE THEORY OF CREATION** which is the **A** to **Z OF THE FATHER GOD ALMIGHTY**.

I AM SELVES COMPONENT

The star from **ME** in the deep of **MYSELF** travels through the Tunnel of Souls, which **I** turn twenty-four hours non-stop and that generates twenty-four hours of non-stop energy. That energy forms the bubbles - spiritual bubbles, which goes *Chiam! Chiam! Chiam! Chiam! Chiam! Chiam! Chiam!* These bubbles go out in the string form of **Os** and spread around into the universal atmosphere to form an object creation. So if a male animal, meets a female animal, they'll produce small animals. If a man meets with a woman they bear and produce another human being. All these are stars that form every living creature and living organisms, and they get their living energies from these bubbles. These bubbles have an Upper Supreme ONE, which is **I THE FATHER MYSELF** in the **SPIRITUAL MANUMITY**. The **SPIRITUAL MANUMITY** is where **I** hide **MY** Nature and nobody knows about it, not even scientists. You will never know, you will never see, and you will never discover. That is **MY BEING** of **MY BEINGS**. So from that point **I** generate **MYSELF** and form AIR and produce the water. When **I** form the water, **I** again generate **MYSELF** as 'The Air' on top of 'The Water' and form the SOUND, the 'GEN' of the Spoken **WORD**, which is **LOVE.** That is what **I** use for the physical creation of everything on earth. However, in that **MANUMITY** the energy, which **I** formulate there, is the **NATURAL SUPREME LIGHT**.

Do you see the sun? Nobody can ever reach there. **I** have two such entities. One is below and the other is above, but the upper one is the sun. No creation can ever reach where the sun is forever and for eternity. None can ever reach there. You have to stop seventy-two millions miles away from the sun. If you pass one inch beyond seventy-two million miles you will burn into ashes – you will melt. **I** put a bar at that point of seventy-two (GB) million miles so that not even angels can ever reach there. It is only **I, THE FATHER GOD THE CREATOR OF THE UNIVERSE** that can be there.

Then when you come to the earth, there's one place the sun meets the earth and comes back. It is called **MATUMA. MATUMA** is where the water vibrates and flows all over the earth and goes back in there. You can see the place, but you cannot get there. Nothing can get close to that place, but there are small, small hollows – that **I** call the **HOLE** and that is where **I** throw all **MY** wastes as the **Earth Hole – *Odu edim Abasi.*** It is actually ***Odu idem Abasi,*** but people call it ***edim Abasi.*** **Edim** in the form of rain means ***idem Abasi*** meaning the body of God or AIR, THE HARDWARE OF THE SUPREME WORD.

You see the rainfall? It is the body of **THE FATHER GOD** called Hardware of God which is hardware of Air. In other words ***k'idem Abasi edioro (that is the body of God).*** In effect, the spiritual self of water is the air, which forms the rain. However the spiritual self of the spirit is the air, which you cannot see. When the air is strong it forms the water and that **Water** is the hardware of the Spirit Air as the Father and Mother of the sound '**THE WORD**'. The Air is the rain; it is also the water. So it is **idem** (body) instead of **edim** (rain). Then **Odu Idem Abasi – Odu** means the **Hole. Odu idem Abasi** means **Hole of the body of God.** This **edim** must fall from the sky when the sun heats it and it melts. When it falls, then all of it will go to **Odu** – that is the **Hole**, which **I** had to put **MYSELF** so that when the water goes back, it has to flow back out again. That is the upper projector of **MYSELF OooOooO**, the Sun which is down on earth to the HOLE. The projector heart of the Sun is **I THE FATHER MYSELF.** From the distance of seventy two million miles of seventy two millions, the Sun travels in projection to form the generator energy to cover the **HOLE-ODU** called **ODU-EDIM-ABASI** and this is what is known as the Atlantic Ocean. When **I** projected **MYSELF** to cover the **HOLE**, the water flowed and **MY HARDWARE** body flowed and that is **ESIT-ABASI (THE HEART OF GOD)**, the Atlantic Ocean and that period became the 'night'. That is **MY** actual meeting point between **MY** Spiritual **SELF** and **MY** Hardware **SELF**. And that is the **SUN** and the **WATER** -The **HEAT** and the **COLD, the MAMA** and **the PAPA.** During this meeting, **I** generate a very tight air and that forms the sound of creation. When **I** finish the meeting, the water flows and goes back into the **HOLE** and this where you see the twelve hours of the day and twelve hours of the night going and coming continuously. The propelling of **MY** force between the tablet Sun in the form ZAKROLL with the pestle and ring of nature is the energy of life for all organisms on earth, whilst, the stimulation or vibration of the meeting produces different forms of nature everyday. And the generation of this force gives energy, which is life to all creations therefore **I AM**

EVERYTHING! THE DIVINE BROTHERHOOD (The bubble of creation) UTIN ODUK ODU-IDIM. ESIT-ABASI, MKPA-OTUN-, AKPA-IYANG-IBOM, THE INNERSELF ENERGY OF ALMIGHTY FATHER GOD.

So **AS I DE MEET, NA SO WE DEY MEET,** and generate the energy of life and produce life force for every of **MY** creations twenty-four hours continuously. **I** would have made this Lecture Revelation a bit more complex, but **I** decided not to. The reason being that **I AM** making it simple for general understanding to demonstrate and counter the Scientists and the philosophers that think they can exist without **ME**, their **CREATOR**. They reason in that manner because they do not consider that everything is part of **ME**. HOW CAN SOMETHING EXIST WITHOUT **ME?** WHATSOEVER YOU ARE, IT IS THE BUBBLE FROM **ME,** AND **I** PUT YOU IN THE POSITION WHERE YOU SHOULD BE, THUS, WHAT YOU WANT

TO BE YOU CANNOT BE BECAUSE **I** MADE YOU TO BE WHAT YOU ARE. YOU CANNOT BE WHAT **I** HAVE NOT MADE YOU TO BE THEREFORE EVERY HUMAN BEING ON EARTH SHOULD UNDERSTAND THIS FROM TODAY AND FOREVER.

In **Odu Abasi,** this is the **HOLE** – just like you have the sun. The sun is in the form of tablet known as **BARDICT – BARDICTIM** format. **BARDICTIM** is like a formulated bar, a formula of bar whereas the 'HOLE' – **ODU** has nothing, it is like a void. One has a platform and the other one has no platform. The one with the platform is the SUN and every living thing can only stop at seventy-two million miles away. If you try to venture close at all, it produces a high-tension energy. If you go one inch beyond the seventy-two million miles you will melt. When you melt, it goes back to **Odu**,-Hole which is *Odu idem Abasi* where **I** send **MY** body back - to regain it in another twelve hours time. This is how the dews form. When the SUN heats and melts the sweat of its energy forms rain, which is the WATER and it also, makes dew to water the creations on earth. The remnant of that dew in turn forms the rain, which is the body of the air, which is **THE FATHER GOD'S HARDWARE**. The SUN produces heat as THE FUEL OF NATURE and then it turns itself to produce the energy that sustains things. That is why the air and the water generate together to produce the energy of physical true life as '**THE SUPREME AIR**' so that things will not die off. This energy of **THE SUPREME AIR** now formulates water again, which is the body of **THE FATHER GOD AIR**. It is like putting fuel in a generator for it to generate energy. If you do not put fuel again the generator will not generate and there would be no energy again. So you put the fuel to generate the generator to give you fuel. **I AM** a **SELF COMPONENT** and **SELF**

COMPARTMENTS as THE GENESIS OF THE GENERATOR.

COMPOUND-CLUDED FATHER GOD

I heat **MYSELF** and produce AIR and COLD and then produce **MY** body as a thick body of the AIR which is WATER. When the AIR melts, it becomes rain and goes back to the **HOLE** and comes back as AIR, and then turns to DEW, which becomes RAIN again and returns to the **HOLE.** That is what is going on twenty-four hours everyday. Twelve hours of cold, twelve hours of heat – the Sun and the Hole.

Now the energy of **HOLE** is COLD and the energy of the **SUN** is the HEAT. Then the COLD and the HEAT put themselves together to produce a **"SOUND"** and that is the child, which is the '**SPOKEN WORD'**, thus all the creation you see are 'Spoken Words'. That is what is called the **FIRST AND THE LAST – FIRST OF ALL –** Brotherhood of all things – **I AM THE**

FATHER GOD. In between all these things that **I AM** explaining to you are messengers, small, small cut-off creations from **B, C,** and **D** and so on and all of them are embedded in the first to last letters that formulate all things, **FIRST OF ALL – AKPAN ABASI -AFRICA,** FIRST **SON OF THE FATHER GOD ALMIGHTY**.

So what we call **Akpan Abasi** is not limited to *owo* (human being) but a human being is a house of **Akpan ABASI** as a symbol. Just like the Ark of the New Covenant is not the box, rather **LOVE** is the Ark of the New Covenant and the box is the symbol. Just as a church of GOD is not the building, rather it is the human being that goes into the building that is the church of GOD. Just as human being is not GOD, but human being is *GOD'S PRESENCE,* because the Spirit of **THE FATHER GOD** lives in a human person therefore that person becomes **GOD'S PRESENT**, but human being is not **THE FATHER**

GOD THE CREATOR OF THE UNIVERSE. Do you understand? So **I AM COMPOUNDCLUDED** everything about **THE FATHER GOD** to form the meaning of **A to Z.**

COMPOUNDCLUDED! Have you spoken that language before? It means putting everything about **THE FATHER GOD** into one **WHOLE,** as a sum total that is **A to Z.** And **A - Z** is **COMPOUNDCLUDED.** Everything that **I AM** going to reveal is incorporated into **A TO Z** Lecture Revelation. Then after the **A** of **A – Z,** B will follow and the next is C and so on and so forth and each of the letters are endless in phenomenon. They are inexhaustibly inexplicable and you cannot explain them to the end of it. This is so because each of the letters is a compound word and linked back to **O.** That is why you can use the letter A to mean anything which is unlimited in meaning. You can also use the letter B to be unlimited in meaning, and this applies to all the alphabets including Z. The Composer/s of the alphabets knows that you can use the letters to compose any number of words and it can mean different things at different times.

THE WIDENESS ANGLE

WISDOM is **MY** first Servant component as everything from **A TO Z** as in **First of Al**l. Listen to this: when **I** had Adam, A - Alpha that had to meet Z, how did **I** make it to meet **Z** of **MY** Spiritual Self which is **ZAKROLL**? How did **I** meet, when **I** went seventy-two millions miles away from **MY** actual Spiritual Self which is **ZAKROLL?** How would **I** go back to meet this one without **WISDOM** which is the letter **W**? Wisdom is the cover energy that links **ME** to cover up to **Z**. That is what is called **THE WIDENESS ANGLE, 'THE WHOLE'**. A wideness angle is anything that can be so wide that it is extensively extending and nothing can be as wide as **WISDOM**. Do you know that is another name for WISDOM? The **WIDE ANGLE, THE WHOLE** is another name for WISDOM which is unlimited in **UNDERSTANDING**. It is so wide that you cannot cover it. Mfon Etteh's body is shaking at all these Revelation Lectures. **WISDOM** is **MY WIDENESS ANGLE** that **I** use to cover the entire **WHOLE** of **MY** physical **SELF** to **MY** Spiritual **SELF** and link back together in three capacities, SPIRIT, SOUL and PHYSICAL TRUTH (**OOO**). It is everything that **I** do. Wisdom is **MY** - *you know, you know,* **MY WIDENESS;** whether you call it Wise, too wise or you call it **WIDENESS ANGLE** or **THE WHOLE**, it is the one that takes **ME** from this angle to the other and again takes **ME** from that angle to the next. That is the one **I** use to cover the space of **MYSELF**. **WISDOM, THE WIDENESS ANGLE** is represented by the letter '**W**' of **A TO Z.** After '**W**' what is the next alphabet? *"It is X."* The day **I** will give the full Lecture Revelation about **"W"** – **WISDOM** which is the Upper Upstairs of **THE FATHER GOD**, **I** will show to you what **A –Z** means. Each of the letters means something that nobody on this earth plane knows, not even angels until **I** decode it. And that is why **I THE FATHER GOD** says that the talent, the spirit, the gift, the blessing that **I** have given to King Solomon David Jesse **ETE**, **I** will never give to anybody. If you give that kind of thing to another person you are in trouble. If you give that kind of blessing to somebody else you are in trouble. You can only give it to yourself. So **I AM THE WIDE ANGLE OF THE UNIVERSE, I AM, THE WHOLE** and **I AM THE PEACE OF THE FATHER** which **Solomon ETE** literally means.

EVERYWHERE, HERE AND THERE

I cover the space. What do **I** use to cover the space? Is it not

WIDENESS? As **I AM CIRCLE** in form, how would **I** do that? If **I** go to this corner, they run away if **I** go to that corner they run away. So **I** take **MY WIDE-ANGLE** to cover everywhere. Anywhere that you are **I AM** there. That is the meaning of **EVERYWHERE, HERE** and **THERE, THE WIDENESS ANGLE** of **THE FATHER GOD** is **WISDOM – THE REASON.** The entire components link to one another and that is why **I** say, '**LOVE ONE ANOTHER**' is the key to everything. If any day letter **A** hates letter **B** he or she is in trouble. Any day letter **B** hates letter **C**, he or she is in trouble. All the component letters which formulate the 'SPOKEN WORD' are one and that is **ME THE FATHER GOD** so you must love each other. **I** do not want to go into all that for now, but what **I AM** doing today is to give you the importance and the meaning of **A** to **Z. ZAKROLL** which is called **ZERO-RING** means **O** which is **Round,** a **Circle** and that is what formulated ALPHA, the Beginning, and

OMEGA the Endingless. Majority of people think that zero-ring is empty. Today the entire creation of humankind knows that ZAKROLL the LETTER 'Z' **ZERO-RING** means the completion, THE OMEGA.

"A" IS EMPTY

When you draw a circle on something and cover the space, can the space be empty? *"No Father."* Do you know what is empty? **A** is empty. That was why Adam was not able to know anything naturally apart from **MY** Holy Spirit in him before he fails, because He was empty. The letter **A** is empty – just as number **one** is alone. When you drag number one like this "**1**"– *kpam,* there is no space, there is nothing inside. Number one is **A**. Its power means to add. **Addition** is the higher self of Adam "**THE SPOKEN WORD**". It is only when you add something to one that it becomes valuable. That is why it is 'at' - A means 'at'. When you say one, it means you must add something to make it meaningful, because it is empty and lonely. What is the meaning of one? What is one? If **I** say **I AM "ONE"**, it means every other thing is not there, but if **I** say **I AM "O" – ZAKROLLS** that means you are included in **ME**. **I** have drawn a circle and you are standing there without knowing that you are inside **ME**. **FATHER OF ALL IS FIRST OF ALL**. **"A"** means first before anything existed. When other things came into existence then it was no more A, it becomes B. The more A increases to B, C, and to D and so on, it becomes more plural. That is why **ALPHA** – Adam was empty and he had to walk from A to B, C, D, and so, so and so up to Z. I've given you this Lecture Revelation before in a different form about the different Brotherhood Degrees. The more he goes up in the component the more he comes back to be **OMEGA** and that makes him become All and All, then He can now rule as The King of Kings and The Lord of Lords with his son.

What could Adam do when he was single? What can a single person do? What can you do if you are single? You have no child. You are a bachelor; you eat *koi-koi-ibeg.* (Tinned food) 'Like *Noodles'.* Noodles are even better, *'Instant noodles'.* Yes instant noodles. However, when you have a son, have a daughter and a friend, it means that A, B, C, D has started.

It is the primary stage of **THE FATHER GOD'S** manifestation that was empty. There was no wisdom and no knowledge. It was afterwards that the journey started. The journey so far, where is that Lecture Revelation on the **'Journey So Far?** Another day **I** will reveal the meaning of **Deep – *mkpotung akpa inyang ibom*** that is the Mother HERSELF. **I** do not want one Lecture Revelation to be too bulky, because it is an endless phenomenon. **I** will leave it so far. When you finish the Lecture Revelation of today and sit down to reason, you will know that **I** have not started anything yet. **I** can upgrade all the things you've heard so far and you won't even need food.

Did you know all these days that **A** is empty and number one is nothingness? Instead of that 'they' say it is the letter O. 'They' turned it upside down and term zero to be nothingness. When they call something zero they term it to be empty. That is Satan's business so that nobody will respect **O-RING**. That is **ZAKROLL,** from the spirit to the physical body. Do you know why it is like that? The carnal people count things from carnal to spirit. Is it easy as that? If nothing exists in spirit, how can it exist here physically? Without **THE FATHER GOD THE CREATOR OF THE UNIVERSE**, there would be no creation of the '**SPOKEN WORD'** and without THE SUPREME **WORD;** there would be no physical creation. Everything, from the beginning was in me; buried in **ME** as **ZAKROLL** and **I**

used **THE WIDE ANGLE - WISDOM** to overcome it. Wide Angle of man and **THE FATHER GOD** is Wisdom. If **I** give you **WISDOM** and **UNDERSTANDING** then you have overcome all your problems in this world, not so? It is **WISDOM** and **UNDERSTANDING** that you take to overcome
all problems, because immediately something happens that will course confusion, you will understand the situation. And with your understanding, you will reason out appropriate answers for the situation. Oh, I should say this or I should not talk or answer; this is what I should do to avoid this misunderstanding, then the problem stops. Conversely, if you do not have **THE WIDE-ANGLE** of yourself, you will give one response that would aggravate the situation and you fight until daybreak or kill yourself because of that simple misunderstanding.

Therefore when **I** give you **THE WIDE- ANGLE** of **MYSELF**, then you are okay. Of course, you need **MY** entire components to be perfectly okay. No one should say I do not want this because I have this. The components are necessary, for you to be a complete child of **THE FATHER GOD** and for **I THE FATHER GOD** to live in you; you must have LOVE with one another. LOVE is what drives on the good will of **THE FATHER GOD** in personnel life. **I** will reveal the energy of **LOVE**. Without WISDOM, you cannot get LOVE and without LOVE, **I** cannot engineer WISDOM in you. Without FAITH, you cannot get LOVE therefore everything links to each other, because they are from one **ZAKROLL** as the First of All of EVERYTHING. First of All and All means **THE FATHER INCLUDED.**

Let **MY** peace and blessing abide with the entire world, in the name of Our Lord Jesus Christ, in the blood of our Lord Jesus Christ, now and forever more. "*Amen!*"

THANK YOU FATHER

Chapter Four

THE SECRET OF THE UNIVERSAL PROBLEMS BETWEEN CHRISTIANS AND MUSLIMS AND THE REMEDY

FATHER'S TALK
(GOD PRESENT)

Noah, Fourth Matthew FATHER Two Thousand and Eight (OD.AA.BOOH) (Tuesday, Fourth November Year two Thousand and Eight (04.11.2008)

In the name of Our Lord Jesus Christ, In the Blood of Our Lord Jesus Christ, Now and forever more

THE SECRET OF THE UNIVERSAL PROBLEMS BETWEEN CHRISTIANS AND MUSLIMS AND THE REMEDY

Second Part of:
ESIEN EMANA AKPAN THE AFRICAN PROBLEM

Today it pleases **ME THE FATHER GOD THE CREATOR OF THE UNIVERSE**, to give this Lecture Revelation, which is the second part of: **AKPAN THE AFRICAN PROBLEM – ESIEN EMANA AKPAN.** The title of this Lecture Revelation is: **THE SECRET OF THE UNIVERSAL PROBLEMS BETWEEN ISAAC AND ISHMAEL (CHRISTIANS AND MUSLIMS) AND THE REMEDY, THE ONLY WAY FORWARD FOR THE WORLD PEACE**

Part One:
THE PROBLEM OF MANKIND

INTRODUCTION:
THE LAUNCHING OF THE UNIVERSAL GREAT CHANGE

I, THE FATHER GOD THE CREATOR OF THE UNIVERSE THE UNIVERSAL SUPREME WORD decided to launch **THE GREAT UNIVERSAL CHANGE** on earth to change things and make things new. It is an operation of natural, spiritual and otherwise gradual processes from many, many generations before now. Therefore, the earlier **I** launched it the better.

THE TWENTY-FIRST CENTURY BELONGS TO THE FATHER GOD ALMIGHTY and is:
The beginning of righteousness
The beginning of goodness
The beginning of joy
The beginning of oneness
The beginning of all good things

This century is **THE BEGINNING OF THE GLORY OF THE FATHER GOD ALMIGHTY**. It is the beginning for **ME** to reap the Fruits of **MY** Creations and to reap the fruits for the reason **I** died for humankind.

TWENTY-FIRST CENTURY BELONGS TO THE FATHER GOD ALMIGHTY and is **THE BEGINNING OF ALLELUIA AND HOSANNA of THE FATHER GOD**. It is also **THE BEGINNING of THE SUPREME FUTURE OF THE FATHER GOD FOR ALL MY POSITIVE CHILDREN**.

For these reasons at the end of the year Nineteen Ninety-nine and the year Two Thousand and the beginning of Two Thousand And One, **I** started the **NEW PROGRAM** called **THE GREAT UNIVERSAL CHANGE.** Consequently, this year **I** launched **THE FATHER'S TALK (GOD PRESENT)** Lecture Revelation titled: *THE GREAT UNIVERSAL CHANGE*, which contains the **INFORMATION** that will change entire of humankind in spirit, soul and the physical.

Before you launch and put up a sure foundation for a new thing or before you build a new house and or renovate an old one, you will first know what the problems are and solve the problems to lay the sure foundation and then launch the new thing.

The Lecture Revelation **I** gave about **ESIEN EMANA AKPAN** titled, *AKPAN THE AFRICAN PROBLEM* in which **I** brought to light that **AFRICA** is **AKPAN** is part of solving the problem of humankind from this year upward.

This Lecture Revelation is titled, **THE SECRET OF THE UNIVERSAL PROBLEMS BETWEEN THE TWO NATIONS (SONS) OF ABRAHAM ISHMAEL AND ISAAC "CHRISTIANS AND MUSLIMS" AND THE REMEDY**. This is also to solve the universal problem. **I** will first of all disclose the root of the problem. That is what **I AM** going to reveal now. Then **I** will add the potency for the **REMEDY** to start to work immediately.

THE ONLY WAY FORWARD FOR THE WORLD PEACE is with **THE FATHER GOD THE CREATOR OF THE UNIVERSE** as the **CORRECT INFORMATION** and also when all humankind listens and accepts the **ORDINANCES OF GOD** and goes back to the **REAL SELF** of **THE FATHER GOD**. All children of **THE FATHER GOD** must resemble **THE FATHER GOD**. All **THE FATHER GOD'S POSITIVE** children must resemble **THE FATHER GOD**, so that they can live with **THE FATHER GOD**

IN UNITY, PEACE AND LOVE. That is the only way forward. **LOVE YE ONE ANOTHER** is the only commandment as **THE BY- LOVE OF WORD IS THE BY LAW OF LIFE 'LOVE YE ONE ANOTHER'.**

I have already sent a **SUPREME LETTER OF LOVE**, which is an invitation of **MY LOVE** to the whole world including all humanity, spirit souls and angels. That is now on. I believe that the distribution of that information, **SUPREME LOVE LETTER** is going on now. So that the whole world would not have any excuse.

Humble yourselves all Christians, all Muslims, all Jews and all other religions. Whatsoever you think you are humble yourself so far as you are a human being, you must read **MY UPDATE** titled *THE UNIVERSAL UPDATE*. There is nothing shielding human beings and spirit-souls from one against the other again, apart from **LOVE ONE ANOTHER. I AM** now going to take away all the barriers and hindrances, but you must accept the truth so that the truth shall set you free. Without accepting the truth you cannot be free and if you are not free, your blood will be upon you.

I have done everything even before the creation and after the creation and now **AM** giving the final blessing so that everyone will live a perfect and peaceful life to carry on for eternity as a **PERFECT PERMANENT LIFE!**

A: **ADAM AND EVE**

As **I** revealed in the first part of this Lecture Revelation '**AKPAN' THE AFRICAN PROBLEM** about **ESIEN EMANA AKPAN, AFRICA** is **AKPAN**. Adam is **AKPAN ABASI** as **THE FIRST OF ALL, THE A** to **Z**. **I** will not dwell too much on this part because **I** have already said everything about it. Nevertheless, **I AM** now about to tell you where the problems all started.

The problems started from Nothingness and also because everything was empty. You can build a house but nobody lives there. You can have a container, but no content in it. You can see the shell of an egg and if there is no egg inside, then you cannot have an egg. You can have a bank, but there is no money in that building called bank. Just as people are happy that the kingdom of God is here because **THE FATHER GOD** has established it but they have not entered this Kingdom of God yet, because many of them are not ready since they refuse to practice simple love to one another.

How can you live in a half-built house, the building that is still in progress? How can you enjoy the food that that has not yet cooked though the ingredients are there? When the food is cooked and the announcement comes that the food is ready then, you can eat. Until then you cannot eat the food when it is still in the process of cooking. Even though the ingredients for the food are available, the dish has not put it together as such; it cannot be termed cooked food. As the food is in process of cooking or preparation of any sort, you cannot be happy that you have food to eat. People jump about saying 'oh this is the Kingdom of God and I thank God that I am in the Kingdom of God.'

THE WHOLE WORLD IS THE KINGDOM OF GOD. EVERYWHERE, HERE AND THERE IS THE KINGDOM OF GOD. I THE FATHER GOD, have established the Kingdom of God, the foundation and all. Everything is in place, but you have not yet entered, because you cannot enter without **LOVE**. There is only one entrance into the Kingdom of God. Why **I** delay, the final judgment is because as **I** see it, **THE KINGDOM OF GOD IS HERE, BUT YOUR POSITION IS STILL EMPTY** because you are not ready to enter!

You wave your hands to be in the Kingdom of God but you are not ready!

You still bear grudges.

You are still annoyed with people.

You still practice demarcations.

You still practice division and segregation.

You still say 'I am brother. I am a man. I am a sister. I am a woman. I am black. I am white. I am a Christian. I am Muslim. I am from here. I am from there. You still see people to be different. You see different groups, categories, sets, subsets, classes, sections and even subsections of human beings, as well as different families of people. You put demarcations and set up boundaries. You still practice separatism and partitioning. How can you have all those divisions in you and say you are in the Kingdom where **THE FATHER GOD** is **ONE**, where **EVERYTHING** is **ONENESS**? What are you coming to do in the Kingdom with all that baggage? You want to come into the Kingdom and cause another problem? Don't fan yourself. You are **NOT** in the Kingdom-o!

If you are in the **KINGDOM OF GOD** then first of all you must **LOVE ONE ANOTHER**.

You **MUST** practice **ONENESS**.

You **MUST** practice **PEACE**.

You **MUST** have **UNDERSTANDING**, **WISDOM** and **HUMILITY**.

You **MUST** practice **EQUALITY** and be **MERCIFUL** and also have the **SPIRIT OF FORGIVENESS** in you. These are the signs that will lead you to the entrance of the **KINGDOM OF GOD**.

So, if you lack these good virtues do not fan yourself that you are in the Kingdom of God. If you think you are in the Kingdom of God then it means that Satan himself will claim that she is in the Kingdom of God because you are working for Satan. If you claim that, you are virtuous, what about the fact that you are jealous of somebody.

What about the fact that 'you' have problems with someone?

What about the fact that 'you' gossip about someone?

What about the fact that 'you' curse people?

What about the fact the 'you' hate people?

What about the fact that 'you' assassinate people's characters?

What about the fact that 'you' are going to soothsayers?

What about the fact that 'you' are doing all sorts of unacceptable things?

What about the fact that 'you' believe in all sorts of things? Thereafter, you claim you re in the Kingdom of God and you have seen **GOD** face to face.

You preach to people, shouting that you are in the Kingdom of God. What about all those characters in you that are inconsistent with what obtains in the Kingdom of God and **THE FATHER GOD**? If you therefore, claim that you are in the Kingdom of God with all those failing characteristics, then it means Satan is the chief there! In that regard **I** categorically denounce that definitely, that is NOT the Kingdom of THE FATHER GOD that **I AM** THE HEAD, THE SUPREME WORD OF THE UNIVERSE, THE DIVINE SELF OF THE FATHER GOD, THE HOLY SPIRIT OF TRUTH WHO HAS PERSONIFIED.

If you are on the side of the Kingdom of God with **THE HOLY SPIRIT OF TRUTH** then first of all **I** will see the fruit of **LOVE**, the fruit of **PEACE**, the fruit of **ONENESS**, the fruit of **TRUTHFUL SPIRIT** and the sign of *LIVE* and *LET LIVE*, especially **PEACE** in you as well as Minding Your Own Business. And **I** will see these fruits in you. **I** will see understanding and wisdom in you. **I** will see the **TOTAL SELF** of **THE FATHER GOD** manifesting in you. Certainly, you will not do all sorts of assignments, invocations and other evil things you do, which are the cunning ways you worship evil and then say you are in the Kingdom of God. Know that by their fruits, ye shall know them!

The first signs of those who are ready to be in the Kingdom of God with **THE FATHER GOD** is **peace, love, humility, truth, oneness, minding your own business, live and let live** and giving **equal treatment** to everybody. Respect your elders, uphold the ordinances of **THE FATHER GOD** and have a good behaviour. If you have, the frame of mind that is that left for you alone there would be no problems in this world then that shows that you are on **MY side.**

As for you, you cause trouble everywhere! You barrier people! You work for evil! You are a member of secret societies. You are a member of cults. You are a member of witchcraft! And then you fan yourself that you are in the Kingdom of God. You are a deceiver. You are all deceivers. That is the reason **I** have come with all these information so that you will not be misled or mislead others.

Test your blood with **THE EVERLASTING GOSPEL** and **the testimony of Everlasting gospel THE FATHER'S TALK (GOD PRESENT)** Lectures Revelations then you will know whether the blood in your spiritual vein is exactly the blood of **THE FATHER GOD,** which means THE TRUTH, THE WORD of **THE SUPREME THOUGHT** which is, **LOVE YE ONE ANOTHER**. Test your blood with that.

Adam and Eve were the first and they had that original problem and that problem generated into all humankind because **the spirit of the first elementary self** disturbed those entities. I upgraded Adam and upgraded Eve so, what about the children of Adam and Eve? You must upgrade yourselves with Love. Did Christ not tell you that without love you would not enter the Kingdom of God? That Christ was the Higherself of Adam talking. Awareness of the **truth**

is **love.** So, now do not say 'I am a child of Adam and Eve, the New Heaven and the New Earth and you do not practice love. If you are in the New Heaven and the New Earth, the Children of **THE HOLY SPIRIT OF TRUTH** then:
    There is no segregation.
    There is no strife.
    There is no arrogance.
    There is no pomposity.
    There is no division.
    It is oneness of all things. LOVE YE ONE ANOTHER and if you have these things then you can proudly say, 'I am also the child of **THE FATHER GOD.'** That old Adam and old Eve have passed away as the old heaven and earth.
    The year two thousand and One and Thousand and Two was the beginning of New Generation.
    The generation of love
    The generation of peace
    The generation of oneness
    The generation of equality
    The generation of everything good

This is the generation of peacefulness, no killing and no death. Any land that continues to kill should, wait and see: **I** will sort them out!
B: **I THE FATHER GOD SPEAKS THE WORD**

MY duty as you are hearing now is to bring out the WORD alive. So that this WORD being the truth shall set, **YOU FREE** and set all human souls free. Now! If you refuse to listen to **THE FATHER'S TALK GOD'S** voice, then your blood will be upon you. **THE FATHER'S TALK (GOD PRESENT)** has nothing to do with the colour of your skin. It has nothing to do with age. It has nothing to do with who spoke them and who did not speak them?

THE FATHER'S TALK (GOD PRESENT) has everything to do with the "**TRUTH**". The VOICE OF GOD IS THE TRUTH. THE VOICE OF **THE FATHER GOD** is LOVE because these are the things that the Voice of **THE FATHER GOD** is concerned with and has nothing to do with the questions such as, 'who did all this talking. Is it a man? Is it a woman? Is it a dark-skin (black) African or light-skin European or American? Is it from a human being of any skin colour in-between? It is a poor man? Is it a rich man?' **I** have swept away all these negative and carnal instincts. What is reigning now is **THE TRUTH**, which is the **WORD OF THE HOLY SPIRIT OF TRUTH** that is in action.

THE FATHER'S TALK is **THE SUPREME WORD OF THE UNIVERSE, THE TRUTH, THE HOLY SPIRIT OF TRUTH, THE COMFORTER.** AND THAT IS WHAT MATTERS NOW!

Therefore, **I THE FATHER GOD** being **THE SUPREME WORD** speaks the **WORD**. When you HEAR the **WORD** and LISTEN to the **WORD** and PRACTICE the **WORD** and HONOUR the **WORD** then, you are on the side of salvation. Without that it cannot work. Therefore, every human being on earth must practice **LOVE YE ONE**

ANOTHER and RESPECT the **WORD**. HONOUR THE **WORD**. Partake in the seasonal celebration of the **SUPREME WORD** through the program of *THE UNIVERSAL SUPREME WORD SEASON CELEBRATION*. And that will show that you have already signed on to **THE FATHER GOD THE SUPREME WORD OF THE UNIVERSE.**

C: CAIN AND ABEL

Since the problem started from the first humans, who was the Father, the natural Adam, the first of all and Eve they passed the same problem to their children **Cain and Abel. Cain and Abel** came out from that same entity as positive and negative, the first and the second.

When you forget reason, reason vexes. Don't forget that in the human way, they try to sort the effect and matter, but they forget to bring on board the cause. Now, **I AM** taking humanity back to the cause of everything so that when you understand the cause then, you understand the cure. When you accept the cure then, the cure eliminates the problem and that is when the problem finally finishes. But if you do not even understand the cause of the problem, how will you tackle it and how will you solve the problem? To that effect, **I AM** now revealing the cause of all these problems.

The cause is "**THE SPOKEN WORD**", THE FIRST OF ALL, and YAK! (LET!) When you refuse that **WORD**, when you don't acknowledge that **WORD** and don't accept that **WORD** then, your problem starts from there. Nonetheless, don't forget that the original problem started from Heaven.

When **I** said to Lucifer to worship The **WORD THE 'AKPAN'**, she refused! And from the time she refused, she became **oxymoron as disagreement spirit.** That refusal prompted all the **AKPAN** indigenes, all the **senior** indigenes, all the truthful self of **THE FATHER GOD** to agree that we should send Lucifer away to the earth. When that spirit was sent away, it became the bad part of **THE FATHER GOD,** the Darkness-self, because it had been sent away from **THE SUPREME LIGHT** because of been sent away from the **LOVE PRESENT OF THE FATHER GOD.** So that Sent Away Spirit soul of Lucifer became the hatred nature. As she came into the world, that spirit of jealousy found a home easily in animals and formed human animal. She established natural hatred and natural jealousy on earth. Through that jealousy, Lucifer deceived Adam and Eve. She used that jealousy to destroy Adam and Eve, because they were empty and easily accommodated it. Then Lucifer through Adam and Eve passed that jealousy to her replica that is, her representative on earth and that was Cain.

Cain became jealous of his brother Abel and killed him. That was the beginning of killing. It is an animal instinct. Killing is animal instinct. Cain killed because he came out from the tribe of **Nothingness, Oxymoron, Disagreement, jealousy** and **death. Hatred** is **death, darkness, and witchcraft** as well as **all evil.** So, that is the meaning of **Cain.**

What is the meaning of Abel and what is the meaning of Adam? What is the meaning of Eve? What is the meaning of Lucifer? All are THE SPOKEN WORD. You cannot see these names, but you hear them because they are WORDS. You can call anything or anybody Abel. You can call anybody Cain but what do you actually mean in calling those names?

It means the pronouncement, the word, the formation and the template. That pronouncement as the WORD is the problem. No human being is the problem.

Nothing on earth is the PROBLEM apart from THE SPOKEN WORD. The WORD became two types. One is positive and the other one is negative.

From there, you have the problem. Conclusively, the problem of everything is The WORD. These WORDS materialized from **ME THE FATHER GOD ALMIGHTY. Evil and negative word means** Satan, good and positive word means God and both systems of words from **ME THE SUPREME SILENT THOUGHT.** And then from the above to **Adam** and **Eve** and from **Adam** and **Eve** the WORDS materialized **Cain** and **Abel**. *THAT IS THE PROBLEM* therefore when you know this truth, the truth shall set you free. That is what it is.

When you know the truth, the truth shall set you free. The truth that shall set you free is for you to accept the truth, **THIS WORD**. And when you accept the truth then that means you are **FREE** because you **UNDERSTAND**. But how could human beings understand what they never heard?

There is lots of information on this earth. Information comes from carnal human beings, from spiritual human beings, from angels, from bible, from this and from that and from all sorts of places, spirit-souls, humans and all but most of the information is mixed. Some of them pass through Angels and you probably would not understand them properly. That is why **I THE SUPREME FATHER GOD ALMIGHTY** HAVE COME NOW, OFFICIALLY TO GIVE THESE RECORDS AND GIVE **THE REMEDY** and TO SORT OUT ALL THE DIFFERENCES in the world through this Lecture Revelation.

Our Lord Jesus Christ, Our Spoken Word, the **WORD** came to the world. **I THE FATHER GOD** was the ONE that became The **WORD** and came to the world. The WORD you are hearing now became human and the flesh died so that that sin will be sorted out. That is why you see **THIS REMEDY** now coming out as the plan of action. Without the **WORD, coming and die for humankind** this would not be possible.

Cain and **Abel** represent the **negative** WORD and **positive** WORD respectively, which **Adam** and **Eve** represented, which **GOD** and **Satan** respectively are as **GOOD** and **ERROR**, **Day** and **night, good** and **bad; front** and **back, up** and **down.** All two, two, twos form the four corners of the universe. But how will you focus attention to your front, which is the side that is good?

Anybody that focuses attention to his or her back is evil. That is the reason evil never walks through the front. They walk through their back. Ask the people that practice evil. If you force any negative spirit to pass through the front, it will melt. That energy will end. They use their backs to walk because they are the BACK of **THE FATHER GOD.** That is the reason witchcraft operates through the back, that is, through darkness. They walk through their back. That is why the sensation spirit of fornication, the energy of evil comes from your legs to your head.

THE HOLY SPIRIT WALKS THROUGH THE FRONT. And The Holy Spirit comes from your head and travels down in you. **I AM** exposing this TRUTH for your benefit. This is not the word of a secret society. It is an open WORD. This is not the word of mystics. It is a TRUE WORD from the Archive Records of **THE FATHER GOD ALMIGHTY.**

I brought them out from the Original Brain, Original Boom, The Computer Memory of **THE FATHER GOD,** The Comprehensive and ability Memory of **THE FATHER GOD;** KING SOLOMON SPIRITUAL LIBRARY.

Therefore, **Cain and Abel** was a Carried Forward problem. Those two tribes formed the segregation on earth.
Cain is **Negative.**
Abel is **Positive.**

D: **ABRAHAM AND HIS TWO SONS**

The problem passed to Abraham the Father of All Nations, and his two sons. **I** do not want to go into all the transits of Adam and Eve.

The Natural Father and **THE SPIRITUAL FATHER** are one. Sometimes **I THE SUPREME WORD** came and lived as a Natural Father to sort out natural things. Then another time **I** came as a **SPIRITUAL FATHER**. **I** first came as a SPIRITUAL FATHER NATURAL, the **WORD** that lived in Adam.

Adam was natural and the **WORD** was spiritual and to separate the two, Cain and Abel came. **Cain** became the **natural** one and he was **negative.** And Abel became the **spiritual** one and he was **positive.** Being the spiritual one, Abel died earlier to form the Holy Ghost.

Since Abel was not a carnal man, he had to go to build a house in the soul world for the spirit soul to live. For that reason, the positive spirit always conquers the negative spirit because that is the CHAMPION SPIRIT, **THE HOLY GHOST OF THE FATHER GOD.**

Abraham was a natural father too, being the incarnate of the natural father. He also came with two sons. One also represented natural, carnal and the other one represented spiritual. The problem again raised its head because of that first nature. It is a very simple thing to understand how this problem of **ESIEN EMANA AKPAN** generates and to see how all these things follow one after the other and cause untold problems in the whole world till today. I do not want to over load this Lecture Revelation because this Lecture Revelation is only part two to *AKPAN THE AFRICAN PROBLEM.* This Part Two is additional information to enlighten you more about the root cause of universal problems so that you understand the whole scenario better.

As human beings are of two types, the natural ones and the spiritual ones presently have differing rates of comprehension, therefore, the carnal people should try to understand this. As for the spiritual people, they already understand what **THE FATHER GOD** means here.

The two sons of Abraham, Isaac and Ishmael represented the same old template. If you are in spirit, you will understand exactly what **I** mean. People fight about that position of **AKPAN** (First son), wanting to be first without considering the problem of **ESIEN EMANA AKPAN,** which is the original problem embedded in **AKPAN** (FIRST BORN SON). When **I** tried to solve that problem through Ishmael and Isaac, it did not work. That same spirit came back there because of the position of **AKPAN** therefore that problem was not solved so, **I** carried forward solving the problem.

The two sons of Abraham were Ishmael and Isaac, but who was **AKPAN** between the two boys since their mothers struggled over that same position and so brought confusion? As the problem of **ESIEN EMANA AKPAN** could not be solved through them at that point, they only established as templates.

You are already familiar with the story of Abraham and the two women in his life, Sarah and Hagar and the two sons.

E: ISHMAEL AND ISAAC

Ishmael and **Isaac** also represented **natural** and **spiritual** respectively. Natural is not evil, but spiritual and natural must grow together.

The **WORD** and the House of the **WORD** and who worships the **WORD**, who speaks the **WORD** and does many other things. In this world, somebody must look after natural things and somebody must look after spiritual things. Those are the things **I** put in place.

Adam was the **Natural Father** and **I** spoke to Adam everyday as a spirit. When Lucifer went and deceived Adam through Eve, **I** cut off and so **I** could not speak to Adam directly again. That made only the **Natural** to remain. Then Satan was able to control **Natural** because he needed an adviser. When you are only, one, alone a lot of things go wrong.

Since Adam became alone when **I** left him, the negative spirit assumed the right to talk to Adam. When you are alone, you think too much and because you think, too much you find it difficult to come into conclusion for better ideas. You are always off and on. Some thoughts would come to you that you would not normally think about if somebody were around you.

For instance, as woman you would not normally think about some men or a man if you had someone around you to talk to but if you do not have someone around you then you would start to think about other men. Your thoughts start to go to some places you have already left when you are alone. That was what happened to Adam.

When Adam sinned directly to the SPIRIT, the SPIRIT did not talk directly to Adam again. Then the negative self started to echo in Adam and directed Adam. That was when problems came. Evil thought which manifested evil words generate evil misunderstanding and that why **elementary self** took over **AKPAN, AKPA AFRICA** (First born) Adam and from then it controlled the whole world. It controlled the world because Adam and Eve passed the lower spirit of elementary self to their children. Then the two children passed them on. That was the same problem that occurred at the time of Abraham with his two children.

Therefore, Ishmael and Isaac, the two sons of Abraham who is **AKPAN** (firstborn son) among two of them, tell me? Who is *udoh* (second son)? Which of the two would **THE FATHER GOD** use to solve the problems of one another? That is the problem **I AM** now talking about, THE UNIVERSAL PROBLEM. **ESIEN EMANA AKPAN** that continued to trouble the whole world until now.

F: **ISAAC AND HIS TWO SONS.**

Since the problem was not solved, it passed to the two sons of Isaac who were Esau and Jacob. Why did that situation happen like that again? Why must it re-occur? Has or did anybody ask such question?

When **I** sent Isaac to be born on earth, **I** gave Sarah to Isaac as a mother who is the natural mother Eve in continuation. Then the other spirit soul brought itself back. He went and brought Hagar from Egypt and put her too in the house of Abraham as a natural woman too. She was also **GOD'S** daughter, but in a different capacity.

I AM telling you this! You have to be very careful! Whenever you see something, you will see another thing and you must be in spirit to conquer that other thing that you see. You must know how to differentiate things. Nevertheless, you MUST love.

I come many times in different ways to solve the Universal Problem through the NATURAL man but no way. I then come as a **SPIRITUAL HUMAN GOD** quite a number of times to live with man and to solve this universal problem during those times. It could not be possible because human beings were not able to carry the task through, because of lack of love one another, lack of understanding and lack of wisdom. Because every human being was the state of elementary self with a very low behaviour, it always spoilt the program.

    You must understand that it is not that **I THE SUPREME FATHER GOD ALMIGHTY** could not solve the problem. The simple reason things seem to drag is that I DO NOT DO ANYTHING BY FORCE. I DO EVERYTHING WITH FREEWILL OF LOVE, because everything established with freewill has root and will stand forever. When you force a situation, it is bound to fall back on your face because there is no root. It is just as a half cooked food that look okay on the outside, but not cooked on the inside therefore, it is likely to cause food poisoning. So, **I** do not want such business again. That is why **I** took **MY** time and arrived with this **CONCLUSION, THE UNIVERSAL PROBLEM AND THE REMEDY** at this time that you are hearing now, this is **THE REMEDY.**

So, Isaac had two sons **Esau** and **Jacob.** Have you asked yourself the question to as whether the problem got solved at that time? It did not solve.

G: ESAU AND JACOB

Natural and **Spiritual** at that point had to live as two brothers. What happened then? The problem did not stop.

When **I** wanted to stop the problem at that point **I** made the two spirits souls to live together and united them so that they will forgive themselves and love each other however the problem came again. What brought the problem back again? **I** will reveal to you what brought the problem.

The problem could not be solved because Esau and Jacob struggled for who should be the first son, the first position as you human beings still struggle today for post and position. Read Lecture Revelation titled ***THE GREAT UNIVERSAL CHANGE, TRUTH, POST, POSITION AND NAME***. These things result in all the struggles in the world by everyone wanting to be the first. 'I should be the firstborn. I should be the first to get there. I should be the first in position. I should be the chairman, the president. I will be the first wife. I am struggling to be the first this and the first that.' You struggle for these things and you still have no remedy for the problems. Is it not true?

Go to the beginning of this Lecture Revelation and check through to see what transpired at those times. Examine the characters of human beings both men and woman and all the things that happened. They are struggled for post and position.

The fisherman and fish: what happen is as soon as the fisherman throws in the fishing rod with a bit of worm or other food to ensnare the fish, the big fish would drive the small fish away, and it will by past it go and swallow that food on the hook. The big fish swallows the food and dies because the fish rushed to that hook thinking it to be good food. Not realizing it is a hook; it swallows it along with the worm and dies.

When you struggle for first the position, you have problems. When you let things go, you would not have problems. Let **THE FATHER GOD** who is ALL and ALL manage the FIRST POSITION, and then you will have no problems.

All human beings on earth, from today, should stop fighting for posts, for positions and to be, for first saying'I should be the first. I should be in control. I should be the leader. I should be a black man or woman. I should be a white man or woman. I should be this. I should be that.' You should stop fighting for all that and humble yourself and live and let live. And if THE FATHER GOD gives you an assignment with, post or position to lead, which is work to be done, you would do it with love for the benefit of everybody. When you stop all that negative elementary-self and misunderstanding, then you are free. That is what you have to understand here now.

Freedom comes from freedom. What is the freedom here? You have no post. You occupy no prominent position; therefore you are free in **THE FATHER GOD** in general. You exist in love, peace and harmony.

As soon as you struggle to take charge of something or people and to lead them, you start to speculate, 'oh I have to be this. I have to be that. I will stand on the left. I will stand on the right.' So, which side is it that is not you? Which side is not **THE FATHER GOD?** Which side is it that is not good?

When you stand on one side, you term the other side to be evil. However, if you stand in the middle and love, then all sides become good. That is what it is, **THE UNIVERSAL REMEDY**, *LIVE AND LET LIVE,* TOGETHERNESS. That is the higher understanding. That is the higher consciousness. **THE REMEDY** is LOVE YE ONE ANOTHER.

Part Two
PRESENT ACTION PLAN

Since the solving of the problem, could not forge ahead because of elementary-self and misunderstanding the situations that surround humankind are about the struggle for who should be the first. They are all about who should be the leader, who should be this and who should be that? I have **AN ACTION PLAN.**

INTRODUCTION: **THE BIRTH AND DEATH OF OUR LORD JESUS CHRIST THE UNIVERSAL SPIRITUAL GOD THE FATHER**

I have to explain to humankind that **MY ACTION PLAN** was the reason I came back on earth in human form, in flesh and blood, not as the natural Self of Adam, but as the spiritual Adam. Our Lord Jesus Christ was the Higherself of Adam. **HE** understood HIMSELF that 'I AND **MY FATHER ARE ONE.**' That **HE** should not claim any, position or claim anything at all. **HE** should just be the Servant, the house of THE SUPREME **WORD** and speak POSITIVE WORDS, establish and practice LOVE YE ONE ANOTHER.

As Adam came back in His Higherself and not in the lower self that was when the problem should have finally been solved because that was **MY FIRST ACTION PLAN** for **ME THE WORD** to come back and 'become flesh and live among men so that humankind's problems should be solved. However, the spirit of '*I am the first* **"ESIEN EMANA AKPAN" that made humans think as** I should control, I should lead, I should be in charge, I should have the lions share as the largest share' still persisted in you HUMAN BEINGS. That stalled progress. That was the work of **elementary self** and that is what is known as **Satan,** which is **the lower self, the lower and**

misunderstanding self. When **I** the **WORD** came and saw those characters still operating, **I** changed the program.

Do you think **I** came on earth to die? Somebody who came to visit HIS OWN WORLD, to reconstruct the world and make things good for people? The death of Christ occurred, because **I** had that plan as **second thought.**

When **I** came as Christ and as the problem was still there the next thing to do was to shed **MY HOLY BLOOD** and have the final potency dropped on earth as **"EVERLASTING FUEL OF LIFE"** to DESTROY the energy of witchcraft the original vampire so that the energy that DESTROYS good things should be finished. That was what **I** was doing at that point and at the same time to give humankind the freedom to pronounce the name of **THE FATHER GOD** openly through the **NAME** and the **BLOOD of OUR LORD JESUS CHRIST**, because in those days when you mention the name of **GOD** they kill you!

They said that when you see **GOD**, you die. That is a lie! It is Satan that is spreading such falsehood. They worship the back instead of worshiping the front.

So, the **FRONT,** which is the LIFE SOURCE as **THE SUPREME SELF** THE FIRST OF ALL became flesh and lived among men and HIS name was **Emmanuel,** whom the Jews called Jesus THE CHRIST. That was **ME THE SUPREME WORD OF THE UNIVERSE, THE HOLY SPIRIT OF TRUTH, THE FATHER GOD** that came as the Higherself of the SPIRITUAL ADAM.

A: **MY PLAN WAS TO END THE PROBLEM THROUGH THE BIRTH OF ISHMAEL AND ISAAC**

At those other previous times, **I** saw that **MY** plan was not going to work. **MY** first plan was to end the problem, through Ishmael and Isaac.

When the two selves were born through Hagar and Sarah as Ishmael and Isaac, both children were in the atmosphere of LOVE ONE ANOTHER. They did not understand what was evil. Their mothers did not have the understanding of their sons, because of the former lower spirit that was still around. Therefore, that deal was not perfect for that time so **I** changed MY PLAN.

What happened then was that Abraham had to offer sacrifice and shifted the program forward. The sacrifice he offered that Isaac was supposed to be the sacrificial lamb meant what? Is it because of what Cain did to Abel? What is the meaning of that? Was that love? That was not love. There was never supposed to be any sacrifice. Sacrifice for what?

Everybody is one and **THE FATHER GOD** is LIFE. Why should this one become sacrifice? Till today people still believe in sacrifice. LOVE ONE ANOTHER IS **THE FATHER GOD'S** ENERGY. You can live with that. Love yourself and love everybody. Do good things. It was the negative self, Lucifer that demanded the LIFE of ISAAC so that positive and spiritual part of ADAM should not continue on earth, just as it demanded the LIFE of ABEL but **I** changed Abel life to through his offer of appreciation mind. But Abel did not live to have a child. The same thing happened to Isaac. Instead of Abraham to sacrifice Isaac, **I THE FATHER GOD** made an improvise to shift the program of solving **THE UNIVERSAL PROBLEM** forward.

B: **THEIR MOTHER WAS THE BARRIER TO THAT PROGRAM JUST AS WAS IN THE TIME OF ADAM AND EVE**

The first people that were the barrier to the program were Sarah and Hagar, the mothers of Isaac and Ishmael. Sarah and Hagar respectively were the first barriers to solving **THE UNIVERSAL PROBLEM** that was brought forward from the time of Adam and Eve.

At that first attempt to launch the program to solve the universal problem, **I THE FATHER GOD** in Natural way brought the two spirit souls together as brothers so that the deal could struck so that **I THE FATHER GOD** would establish peace. There was a reason for the girl Hagar that became the mother of Ishmael to come from Egypt. There was a reason for that. She gave birth to the first child so that first instinct of the first thing passed on to that first child Ishmael to represent his natural father, Abraham. That was why **I** first locked the womb of Sarah so that eventually when Abraham had finished with his physical energy which is the blood of the natural man, and then bring his spiritual self through Isaac. That was exactly what **I** did, so that it will be natural human being and spiritual human being living together in love, unity and peace as Brotherhood of the same parent.

Isaac was born when Abraham and Sarah were very old. Instead of the women understand this action, as the whole world refused to understand the ways of The SPIRIT till today, they went into jealousy and struggled and quarrelled about whom should be the first? Does it matter who is the first? Problems are there, facing you like all the killing, death, lack of peace and many other ills of society but there you are talking about who should be the first and the second.

Sarah and Hagar did not talk about loving one another. They did not discourse how the two children should be taken care of very well. They did not consider who and what should make them happy. They did not think about peace that should reign supreme in the world or contemplated about everlasting life.

Since they refused to understand all that and so would not consider what mattered, they caused that program not to work. They were the barriers to the program and so things ended as they did. That is why you see Muslims and Christians fighting till today.

The fighting of Muslims and Christians till today is not because somebody or groups of people of today caused the current fighting. What is responsible is the template. It is the struggle for who should be **"AKPAN" FIRST SON,** who should be **"UDOH" SECOND SON.** The *hatred* and *jealousy* you are practicing in the house of your father Abraham are the root cause of all your problems.

Are Christians and Muslims not still brothers?

Did they not come from the same father?

Christians and Muslims; are they not human beings?

Are they not from Adam and Eve originally?

Are they not from Abraham?

The loggerheads and struggles between Sarah and Hagar, the two mothers of Ishmael and Isaac were because the two mothers' spirit was involved in the creation of human beings from the beginning.

Lucifer was a female part of **THE FATHER GOD.** When she was banished to earth, she was jealous and came and used the serpent male organ, the natural animal instinct to have a way in Eve. That became two fathers and two mothers and they brought Cain and Abel physically on earth. That established the two templates.

So, to solve the problem at that point, this same spirit of jealousy of Lucifer surfaced again. Hagar and Sarah displayed the same spirit of jealousy, because of that first spirit of jealousy. They quarrelled and had misunderstanding and confused Adam again, who was then Abraham; it was the same natural Father Adam. As a result the same death, hatred, lack of love and lack of peace in the world continued. That was the first barrier from the mothers. The two mothers were the downfall of Ishmael and Isaac and that is why in the Islamic nations they do not give respect to women, because women are full with jealousy and they are quarrelsome.

C: MY PLAN WAS TO END THE PROBLEM THROUGH ESAU AND JACOB

MY Program Was To End The Problem Through Esau And Jacob. Esau and Jacob were the children of Isaac, the same representation of the father Abraham. Did the program work then? You will hear in the next subtitle the reason the program did not work.

You must have deduced that the program did not work through the two brothers. Everybody is familiar with the story of Esau and Jacob. You know the cause of that problem.

When the children were not yet born, the prophecy came that the senior shall serve the younger. Why should the senior serve the younger? **I** put that in place because **I** wanted to solve the problem of **AKPAN** (first son), which is **ESIEN EMANA AKPAN** that is still disturbing people and making people to suffer till today.

As the **MASTER PLANNER, I** gave that stipulation for a good outcome. However, humanity, being very low in mentality did not understand **MY** action. That also constituted the problem.

D: **THE SECOND BARRIER**

Who was the second barrier? The mother of Esau and Jacob was the second barrier to the execution of the program to solve the universal problem. Just as Sarah and Hagar, were the barrier at the time of Abraham, Rebecca the mother of Esau and Jacob became the barrier again for that problem not to be solved.

When **I** said **I** wanted to bless Esau and so solve **AKPAN** problem, which would have brought an end to the problems of the whole world today, their mother craftily presented Jacob who received that blessing instead of Esau and so that **ESIEN EMANA**

AKPAN still remained with Esau who was **AKPAN OR AFRICA.** The problem was not solved then and so **ESIEN EMANA AKPAN** still disturbed Esau as **AKPAN** (first son or first position).

You have to understand that it was not Jacob that wanted to usurp his brother's position. Jacob did not want to do that. Just like Isaac who loved Ishmael. He did not want to take the position of **AKPAN** (first son) from Ishmael because he wanted to solve the problem once and for all. But their mothers did not agree for that to happen. It was that **ESIEN EMANA AKPAN** nature, the animal nature, the serpent instinct, the vampire, that was responsible for that. Who then, is the root problem of **ESIEN EMANA AKPAN or AFRICA?** It is the lower part of God's creations with their *low mentality* if you don't know, know it today, among the **FOUR LIVING CREATURES,** namely fish, bird, animal and human, human being who was created last, they were all sons and draughters of God in the circle of Brotherhood. Therefore, do not forget that fish, bird and animal are the senior creation to the natural human God that I created last on the fifth day. Therefore the lower natures, but first in position of creation are the problems of this world, because they lack understanding and love. They have no mercy, they have no spirit of wisdom and peace, they have no spirit of unity and oneness therefore they are carnal, weak and of a low system of nature that are developing to become like human beings in nature. That is why there is this general and universal notion that women are the cause of problems in the world. It is not the women that are the problem per se, but the nature in them, which is **disagreement** with its component of lack of humility, lack of love, lack of peace, lack of understanding and lack of wisdom, I mean the actual original nature of a woman the lower NATURE.

The problem comes from when you marry a woman and she has a child with you. When that woman disobeys you and goes away, she indoctrinates your child against you just to spoil you in the eyes of your son and also to create the impression that the break down of the marriage was not her fault, even though it may have been. So, spirit of jealousy would be in full operation here.

The Spiritual problem of divorced parents in nature is the root cause of **AKPAN'S** problem and all the problems of the entire world till today.

What is the meaning of throwing Lucifer to earth? Is it not divorcing that spirit? Lucifer was divorced from Heaven. So, she used that divorced spirit and came and disturbed the earth and caused problems for Adam. And that problem led to the rest of the problems of the world till tomorrow unless you address the issue now following this information.

If you would not accept to be with **ME THE FATHER GOD ALMIGHTY** from today to allow **ME**, THE **NEW FATHER AND** MOTHER GOD who is

THE HOLY SPIRIT OF TRUTH to take control and solve your problems then, you will continue to suffer.

THE HOLY SPIRIT IS THE **TOTAL POTENCY** OF **THE FATHER GOD,** THE FATHER, SON AND THE HOLY SPIRIT. It is not **THE FATHER,** SON AND THE MOTHER again. **THE BLESSED MOTHER, THE *ABASI MU-UDIM*** IS WITH THE HOLY SPIRIT OF TRUTH. Everything has become ONE.

It is no more **FATHER, SON** and **MOTHER,** but **FATHER, SON** AND **THE HOLY SPIRIT.** That is UNITY. Everything becomes LOVE, because you cannot take it away. That is why Our Lord Jesus Christ being **THE SUPREME WORD OF THE UNIVERSE** became THE MEDIATOR.

THE MEDIATOR means the one that came and be in the middle to solve the problem of Father and Mother, the spiritual self and natural self to understand each other.

In this world, the problem human beings have is that **spiritual people** do not understand **carnal people** and vice versa that is, **carnal people** do not like **spiritual people.** That is the root of all the problems and the entire killing you see today in the world. Nevertheless, THAT **MUST** STOP! IT **MUST** STOP! The **natural** and the **spiritual** MUST live together, be it carnal or spiritual you must live together in Unity Love and Peace. There is no fighting and killing anymore!

The second barrier not to solve **THE UNIVERSAL PROBLEM** was Rebecca the mother of Esau and Jacob. She put up the barrier for that deal not to work through her deceitful action of swapping the blessing that was for Esau *(AKPAN)* to Jacob *(UDOH)*. As a result, the problem still continued. Just as Sarah and Hagar were the barrier for the problem to stop between Ishmael and Isaac. Just as Lucifer's barrier did not allow Adam and Eve to wait until **I** sort the problem, which was for them to wait until **I** blessed the fruits before they ate. And so they passed that problem to Cain and Abel as they ate the fruit without **MY** blessing it.

E: MY NEXT PLAN WAS TO END THE PROBLEM THROUGH JACOB AND JOSEPH.

When Jacob was born, he received the blessing from his father through the cunning of his mother. Then eventually, **I** brought Reuben and his eleven brothers making them twelve brothers altogether. And amongst them was Joseph whom **I** specifically brought so that the universal problem that is between the **father** and the **mother** would be solved.

Joseph had a dream that he saw the sun and the moon and the twelve stars. That eleven of the stars bowed down for one of the stars. And also, he saw the sun and the moon bow down as well for that particular star. That showed that Joseph was God amongst them. **I THE SUPREME WORD,** manifested **MYSELF** through

Joseph to solve the problem in the House of Jacob, which was the Tribe of God. **THE UNIVERSAL PROBLEM** still continued. Who caused yet another barrier here?

Reuben and his brothers were the culprits at that period.

F: **THE THIRD BARRIER**

They did not allow that plan to work. They lured Joseph to the field to kill him. They did all sorts of things to bring the demise of Joseph. They really planned to kill him. So, the family members, Joseph's brethren became the problem not to let that assignment work in order to solve **THE UNIVERSAL PROBLEM** once and for all. To avoid disaster and destruction **I** ended things as they did during that era. As you probably know, the children of Israel endured forty years of slavery in the hands of Egypt. Therefore, you should now realise that all the past struggles did not bring civilization and any good thing to anybody. Without love, you still struggle. This WORD of LOVE, which is the **REMEDY,** is what **I** have been preaching about and talking about. You have NO reason to refuse this WORD of LOVE now because The Holy Spirit has taken control.

As the brethren starting from Reuben caused the barrier to that blessing, who was Reuben is it not **AKPAN**? **I** left things as they were. So, the program to sort the problem still continued.

G: **THE FINAL ACTION PLAN THE BIRTH AND THE DEATH OF CHRIST**

Therefore, to cut the long story short, **the Birth and the Death of Our Lord Jesus Christ** was **The Final Action Plan** to bring the final remedy back on earth. It was due to all those barriers at various times that made **ME** have the **Second Thought**, which is why **I** said at the beginning of this Part Two that there was nothing else **I** could do than to die for humankind so that, that would bring the **REMEDY** and would bring love and peace. The action would also establish love on earth again. That was the **Final Action Plan that I Put in Place.**

After the death of Christ, everyone became one. No Jews, no gentiles, no Christians, no Muslims, no Judaists, no religion. NO DIVISION at all. EVERYBODY HAS BECOME ONE!

WHO IS CHRIST? Christ is the **FATHER** of Ishmael and Isaac. Even till today as **I AM** talking now, the Muslim world does not understand that Jesus Christ they do not want is their Father Abraham who was Adam, because they do not understand and believe the system of Incarnation, Reincarnation and De-incarnation. Jesus Christ was ADAM'S Higherself, with the full Supreme energy from the time of creation; He was the higher consciousness of ALL **THOUGHTS**. If Muslims and Christians knew this, they would not kill each other. **I AM telling you that this is THE ABSOLUTE TRUTH;** *this information is not from an angel and is not second hand information*. That is why you should no more believe that Christians are different from Muslims or that Muslims are different from Christians. The same natural Father and Mother and the same spiritual Father and Mother are the original Parents of the two nations. **I THE FATHER GOD, THE CREATOR OF THE UNIVERSE, THE UNIVERSAL SUPREME WORD** is your **FATHER GOD,** and **I WANT THAT PROBLEM TO END NOW, THE PROBLEM OF AKPA/ AKPAN, AFRICA, THE PROBLEM OF CAIN AND ABEL, THE PROBLEM OF ISHMAEL AND ISAAC THE FIRST OF ALL TO END NOW. THIS IS THE STARTING GENERATION OF THE SUPREME FUTURE OF THE FATHER GOD therefore I WANT EVERYONE TO LIVE IN UNITY, PEACE AND LOVE AND IF THERE IS ANY**

NATION THAT WILL NOT HEAR THIS WORD OF LOVE, UNITY AND PEACE, I THE SUPREME NATURE WOULD WIPE-OUT THAT ROOT COMPLETELY FROM THE SURFACE OF THIS EARTH FOREVER.

I want understanding to be established now in all nations of the world. **Christ** is a language. **Christ** means the **Anointed One.** I elevated the spirit-soul of Adam to be higher so that when Adam came back **I THE SUPREME WORD** that did not have anywhere to live should live in Adam as Jesus Christ, the Higherself of Adam. **JESUS CHRIST IS THE GOD OF HEAVEN AND EARTH, THE CREATOR OF THE UNIVERSE** in spirit, but in the physical truth, He is **THE SPIRITUAL ADAM, THE FATHER OF ALL HUMAN BEINGS, THE KING OF KINGS AND LORD OF LORDS, THE FATHER OF ALL NATIONS. HE** was born on earth through the Holy Spirit. HE was the spiritual Adam that came to salvage HIS children and to help all the souls of the natural fathers that were actually HIMSELF in a natural way, namely Adam, Abraham, David and so on and so forth.

You can see that when Our Lord Jesus Christ came on earth, HE did not have anything to do with any woman so that there would not be another problem. Even at that, they still brought women into the matter.

Mary Magdalene stood there.

Martha stood there.

Many other women stood there. To do what? What are they looking for in the first place?

They were there to try to frustrate the effort again. They could not succeed to frustrate the plan because Jesus Christ was not conceived in a human manner. If Jesus Christ were conceived in a human way, Mary Magdalene, Martha and all of those other women would have put hands together to frustrate that program again.

Till today, many people unfortunately do not believe that

Jesus Christ was conceived through the power of the Holy Spirit. They refused to accept that the Virgin Mary did NOT sleep with any man to get pregnant with Christ. They thought it was impossible for such to be. Nevertheless, **I THE FATHER GOD, AM** telling you that the birth of Christ did not have anything to do with any human blood. That is the reason when anybody died it does not have effect as the death of Christ because the Birth of **CHRIST** was the **TOTAL WORD OF GOD. CHRIST WAS THE TOTAL WORD PERSONIFIED ON EARTH.**

HIS conception did not have anything to do with human blood apart from HIS development inside HIS mother's belly, who was a virgin. The reason Mary the Mother of Christ had to be a virgin was so that no generation seed would be part of HIM (Christ). If any generation seed were to be part of CHRIST, HE would not have resurrected when HE died because it would have meant HE died with sin.

So, when Abel confirmed 'This Is The Holy Ghost', he was the Dove of God, the first innocent person that died and became the Holy Ghost. He was the positive part of his father Adam, the First House. That WORD had to confirm HIS SPIRIT, THE **WORD** and said, "HEAR YE HIM THIS IS **MY** BELOVED SON". That was the deal, and the Ghost that said, **"HEAR YE HIM THIS IS MY BELOVED SON."** That meant that the blood of Christ would salvage humanity, because HE had nothing to do with a human blood. When Jesus Christ eventually died when HE was crucified on the cross HE (CHRIST) then resurrected and took the darkness away from the Paradise of **THE FATHER GOD.** That was **THE FIRST SPIRITUAL REMEDY** that **I THE FATHER GOD** succeeded to put in place as **THE CHAMPION** for the whole world. Nonetheless, that was in the spiritual-soul. That is why people say that after the death of Christ Satan still controls the world. *Na lie!* That is indeed false. Where is it that Satan that controls?

Now, if anybody died in Christ anyone who has no blood in his or her hand, the person will resurrect after seventy-two hours that is, three days and three nights and would take a new body and the person's life continues. You can now progress. Previous to the death of **CHRIST,** it was that when you died you stayed there in prison, in the dark.

The reason Satan imprisoned all those that died, was because the more you come and go, the more you become higher in understanding. It is just as you attending school in the physical world to acquire knowledge. The more you study and progress higher in your education and studies the more knowledgeable you are and the better you are. Similarly, you attain higher consciousness that is, Higherself as you go and come back on earth. But if you are detained when you die, your chances of learning is no longer available because it is cut off. And that means you cannot go higher in education.

So, when people died and could not resurrect that is, reborn back on earth to take the higher evolution to know things, the world continued to be in darkness. That is the reason that the world progressed better from two thousand years ago from when Christ died, compared to periods before the death.

People now know that it is not good to kill. It is not good to segregate. It is not good to cause division. People now know the meaning of LOVE. The WORLD from that time after the death of Christ became ONE, more and more. That is why you see America, Britain and everywhere else in the world talking about ONE WORLD, ONE UNITY and ONE UNDERSTANDING! Eventually the whole world will become one. Now you can see a **solid-skin** or **dark-skin** human (Blackman) and a **soft-skin** or **fair-**

skin humans (Whiteman) stay together. It never was like that previously. Before the death of Christ, none of them could stand each other. Nobody could stand anybody. Everybody was operating 'cut and join' mode of living. But today! The blood of Christ removed all those hindrances. Since Christ destroyed that darkness, that spirit of darkness, the Hades and took upper hand, then that soul part of the problem became solved forever. Now, **I THE HOLY SPIRIT OF TRUTH** HAS COME BACK FOR THE FINAL ASSIGNMENT, which is to solve the physical part of the whole matter because in spirit there is no problem anymore. That is why **I** brought that Lecture Revelation titled *AKPAN THE AFRICAN PROBLEM,* which is *ESIEN EMANA AKPAN.* **THE HOLY SPIRIT OF TRUTH** HAS COME TO SOLVE THE PROBLEM ONCE AND FOR ALL.

That was the Plan.

THE BIRTH AND THE DEATH OF CHRIST BROUGHT SALVATION AND

UNITY TO ALL SOULS, IN THE SOUL FORM. Now, it is the time to join it with the PHYSICAL **REMEDY.**

Part Three
THE REMEDY

THE CONCLUSION

INTRODUCTION: **THIS IS YOUR LAST AND FINAL CHANCE**

As **MY** plan for the program succeeded and Light penetrated into Hades, it became the light of **THE FATHER GOD**, HOLY GHOST and so there is no darkness anymore. That is why if you die in your witchcraft practices or in any wicked and negative way you become an evil ghost, and if you were a killer before you died, you will come back to commit suicide so that your blood will be upon your hand. Some bad and evil teaching said that if you kill you will go to heaven. It is not true! Since your father and mother killed and did many evil things on earth how many of them you see in the heaven. That word is from Satan so it will have company in the hell, because as far as **I THE FATHER GOD** is concerned if you hate or kill any soul you are in the hell, and the sign that will follow you is that you will come back to kill yourself by yourself. This is so that in the last judgment day nobody will answer for your blood.

Previously when people died they would not come back because evil still ruled them. However, after the death of Christ all the souls starting with Adam, Abraham, David and all other souls are released and they became free in the paradise of souls, so they parade and became established for good. If you do good things now and it happens that you die or you went on spiritual transfer to the great beyond, it will take only seventy-two hours and you will come back to continue with your job. You can now speak well for a better tomorrow.

Whatsoever you want tomorrow in regards to future wealth of life and well being and any positive word for your soul evolution, speaks it now and keep the seal in your record. Register your party in spirit now with **ME**. What is your party?

Your party is LOVE YE ONE ANOTHER.

What is your party?

Your party is goodness, mercy, kindness, peace and honesty. Join any of these of Parties of **THE FATHER GOD.** Join any of these positive selves of **THE FATHER GOD.** And when you come back to the earth, you will have no problems again.

THE REMEDY IS THE SPOKEN WORD, THE TREE OF LIFE. Think good thoughts. Speak good words. Hear good words, see good things and do good things.

Think well, speak well, hear well, see well and do well.

A: **I HAVE FINALLY COME OUT TO SPEAK OPENLY TO ALL HUMANKIND**

Now **I** can speak openly to all humankind that **I AM THE SPOKEN**

WORD THE CREATOR OF THE UNIVERSE, THE SUPREME WORD. You must all celebrate during *THE UNIVERSAL SUPREME WORD SEASON CELEBRATION*.

As ETE ROYAL UNIVERSAL FAMILY of this world represents the ORIGINAL NATURAL FAMILY OF **THE FATHER GOD** and THE HEAVENLY FAMILY has also established here on earth, so THE TABERNACLE OF GOD IS WITH MAN NOW. That is why you see:

THE HEAVENLY FAMILY OF THE SUPREME WORD IS HERE. And **THE NATURAL FAMILY OF THE FATHER GOD** IS HERE.

THEREFORE, ADAM AND EVE ARE HERE!

THE HEAVENLY FATHER IS HERE!

THE HOLY SPIRIT IS HERE!
THE TRINITY GOD IS HERE!

So, THE **TRIBE** OF **THE FATHER GOD** IS NOW ESTABLISHED ON EARTH, THE KING OF KINGS AND THE LORD OF LORDS OF THE UNIVERSE.

Now YOU! Every human soul must accept this final arrangement. Nobody is **AKPAN** again and nobody is **UDOH** but only **THE FATHER GOD.** Everybody is under Christhood. You are all under your Father THE KING OF KINGS AND THE LORD OF LORDS that is, LOVE YE ONE ANOTHER.

There is no Muslim separation.

There is no Christian separation.

EVERYBODY IS ONE UNITY, LOVE AND PEACE.

You can call yourself a Muslim. It does not matter.

You can call yourself a Christian. It does not matter. Nonetheless, don't forget that you are one from the same Parent.

What is the meaning of Muslim? Muslim is **GOD WORD** from Abraham and his son Ishmael, which Abraham was a copy of the same natural Adam. What is the meaning of Christianity? Christianity is the total Positive **GOD WORD** from Abraham and his son Isaac, which Abraham was a copy of the same natural Adam. All children of

Abraham are from one father. However, one is spiritual. One is natural. As we have **Spiritual Father**, we also have **Natural Father**. The **Spiritual** and **Natural** must live together for progress. From the natural, we have spiritual. From the spiritual, everything becomes one.

CHRIST MEANS THE KING, ANOINTED ONE. Christ does NOT mean a church leader.

Christ does NOT mean the leader of an organization. Christ does NOT mean a leader of a religion.

Christ does NOT mean a leader of race.

All human beings are from one race. That one race is Adam and Eve, unless of course you are an animal. Even if you are animal, but you took evolution to become a human being, you have then signed on for Adam, the final GOD THE FATHER, and THE CHRIST OF GOD. Adam is the Father of all races of humans. HE IS THE KING OF KINGS AND THE LORD OF LORDS FROM GENERATION TO

GENERATION. That is the TRUTH AND THE SAME THING.

It is only the language, the slips of tongue that confused people. People say this is Christian and this is Muslim. So, who is not Adam? **I ASK YOU**?

I have used the DEATH OF CHRIST to forgive all mothers for what they did and all **AKPAN. I** have subdued all elementary spirits. I said, "*IT IS FINISHED*" on the cross. And truly, IT IS FINISHED!

People say after the death of Christ Satan still tempts people. People still kill themselves. People still fight. Yes, they fought then, but **NOW** the fighting has ended, **I HAVE STOPPED THE FIGHTING AND KILLING NOW AND FOREVER**, IN THE **NAME** AND **BLOOD** OF OUR LORD **JESUS CHRIST. ENYE! ODUDU ABASI MI OOO ZIM ZIM ZIM ASSASSU POSITIVE POSITIVE POSITIVE**. AMEN!

If you do not end your fighting now, you will commit suicide and die and your blood shall be on you.

B: THE PROBLEM OF THE FIRST NATURE IS NOW OVER THROUGH THIS LECTURE REVELATION OF ESIEN EMANA AKPAN CALLED 'AKPAN THE AFRICAN PROBLEM'

IT IS ENDED! It ended from the day Christ entered into the Hades and killed the darkness spirit soul and that was the hatred. Don't you hear? LOVE means LIFE! HATRED means DEATH!

What made you to carry a knife and kill people and to use bomb to kill people? It is that spirit of darkness.

Therefore, if you want to fight somebody, fight death fight hatred. You cannot fight human beings and say you are fighting hatred. Human beings are the houses of hatred and the houses of love. So, use the SPOKEN WORD now. Celebrate **THE SUPREME WORD.** Partake in *THE UNIVERSAL SUPREME WORD*

SEASON CELEBRATION, which is a yearly celebration for eternity.

All governments of this world, if you want to fight terrorists, if you want to fight evil, if you want to fight any problems at all, fight hatred. You cannot however, fight hatred with bullets or with any other physical thing. You can only fight hatred with the spirit of **UNITY, LOVE AND PEACE** and that is by partaking in ***THE UNIVERSAL SUPREME WORD SEASON CELEBRATION.*** By also loving one another, maintaining peace, practicing Live and Let Live, bringing everybody together and recognizing **THE FATHER GOD THE CREATOR OF THE UNIVERSE,** THE PERSONIFIED **WORD** now on earth as the final Adam, THE KING OF KINGS AND THE LORD OF LORDS **OOO**. By recognizing **HIM** and stop, causing confusion by saying **HE** is not GOD and that man is not GOD, but God in man is THE SUPREME WORD that does everything physical on earth. What is man, if man is not GOD?

If man, is not GOD what is man then? If man, is not The KING of Kings and The LORD of Lords, who then is The KING of Kings and The LORD of Lords?

The **WORD** lives in man. Every human being is a young, young God that is, all human beings are small, small Gods. The portion of the **WORD** lives in you. Whomever **THE SUPREME WORD** resides in and personifies that person is The **God of the Earth**. That person is **God the Father. THE FATHER GOD** is The SPIRIT, **THE SUPREME WORD** that manifested to be **God the Father.** Then you have **THE FATHER GOD, GOD** and **God the Father** and that is **Trinity,** Man in three capacities on earth. So, where are you going to throw away this information, this TRUTH? And what are you going to believe again?

If any human being would not believe this information, what are you going to believe? Are you going to have faith and believe in something that has no life? Are you going to believe fighting terrorist with bombs? Are you going to believe fighting wars and killing one another? Since you have been fighting all sorts of wars, where has it led you? Where it has led you is that you leave behind enemies for you children and their children's children. If any head of a country fights terrorist with bombs, they declare open enmity with others for their people. Wars are still going on in the world. All these wars will end through all these good things **I** put in place. That is the shortest cut to war. Moreover, the physical war is too tedious. You go through sufferings, sustain injuries including incapacitation, lose of limbs and other parts of the body, maiming, lots of killing, both mental and physical stress...name them. These have been going on for ages and generations. But now through the death of Christ all that has ended because HIS death made possible the physical manifestation of The Holy Spirit.

Now, THE HOLY SPIRIT IS HERE ON EARTH PHYSICALLY and has brought THE FINAL **REMEDY** and that is, LOVE YE ONE ANOTHER. Celebrate **THE SUPREME WORD** by partaking in ***THE UNIVERSAL SUPREME WORD SEASON CELEBRATION.*** This means to celebrate The **WORD** in you. Don't kill any animal or human being. Don't hurt any human being. LOVE ONE ANOTHER. Practice oneness, kindness, righteousness, which is also honesty, be merciful and be peaceful. Practice peace. Think well, speak well, hear well, see well and do well.

All governments on earth should attach themselves to this information.

If you are a president, practice love and unite everybody. Let your campaigns be with love, in peace and in oneness. Do not create bomb. No government of this world should use the country's money to create bomb, nuclear weapon or any killing things.

If anybody plans to kill or kills, when that person is caught, send the person away to that area kept for people like them. And such a person will never see this side of the world again. Do not kill the person. Such a person would stay banished to that area and would die naturally there. He or she would die by their natural planned death. So, do not involve yourself with any blood.

When this practice progresses on and on, on earth, there would be jubilation of love, of practical oneness and the practice of LOVE ONE ANOTHER. Everyone would also participate fully in **THE UNIVERSAL CELEBRATION OF THE SUPREME WORD SEASON,** which is a yearly celebration for eternity. Then, **I** WILL SPRAY **MY SPIRIT** INTO ALL FLESH! As **I AM** talking now **I** HAVE ALREADY SPRAYED THE **POTENCY OF LOVE** ALL OVER THE UNIVERSE. If you plan evil to any human soul, you will see **CAPITAL *PUNISHMENT!*** You will receive the severest repercussions for your evil plan.

C: **ALL NATIONS OF THE WORLD ARE ONE**

Africa is one. Europe is one. America is one. Asia is one. Everywhere, here and there is one and the same place and one person of our Father ADAM. In the whole world, I have three things, spirit, soul and physical.

You must live in spirit and that is the understanding of the Higherself, which is LOVE ONE ANOTHER. To live in soul means anything you practice, anything you do with your hands, your energy, any good ideas...like scientists that invent things and make innovations to make life and living comfortable. That is good in the form. Things like the discovery of electricity, invention of airplanes to convey people to and fro everywhere in the world and many other things that makes life easy so that there is no more suffering in that area of living. For instance, you do not need to walk from Europe to Africa or to anywhere.

The world expanded and the expansion makes distances far. As **I** expanded the world, **I** came through as the SCIENCE to develop all sorts of things to make life easy. You do not need to take pride in yourself that you are the one that discovered those things or invented anything because it is the **WORD** that lives in you that did that. Any day you finish with that assignment, the WORD changed and started living in another house. That is why sometimes you see people just drop dead. Nevertheless, you do not die because your idea still exists. That is the soul. Then physically is the physical house.

 I advise everyone to go through at least seven **FATHER'S TALK (GOD PRESENT)** Lecture Revelations then you will know yourself. The Lecture Revelations are not something that you need another person to read and preach them to you. Pray to **ME THE FATHER GOD** and the **HOLY SPIRIT** of **THE FATHER GOD** will activate in you and then when you read any of

THE FATHER'S TALK (GOD PRESENT) Lecture Revelations you will understand.

All nations of the whole world are one. There is oneness between Adam and Eve, between Abraham's sons Ishmael and Isaac and between Esau and Jacob. Everyone in the whole wide world including Africans, Europeans, Asians, Americans, Australians and all, are all ONE IN CHRIST meaning, ONE in **THE FATHER GOD, EVERYTHING ARE BROTHERHOOD**.

When you hear the name of Christ, do not say it is not Muslim. Christ means The KING of Kings and the LORD of Lords. And who is that KING? HE is your father Abraham the same natural copy of **ADAM.** Do you think **I** called any person the **FATHER OF ALL NATIONS AND ALSO CALLED HIM MY FRIEND,** who is **DAVID?** Do you think **I** called any person **MY LORD AND CALLED JESUS CHRIST THE SON OF DAVID AND ALSO CALLED HIM MY BELOVED**? Unless of course you want to fight your father then, go ahead. You have been fighting your father and that is the cause of the untold problems you have till today.

When you killed, whom did you actually kill? You killed yourself. Some people say when you kill a Christian or Muslim you will go to heaven. Na lie, pure lie you are rather going to hell, because **I** have been in the **HEAVEN** for how long now and I **have** never seen any sinner coming close to **MY** door of HEAVEN talk about a killer of the word! That is absolute falsehood! It is total fallacy! That is outright misconception!

Who are the Muslims or Christians you are killing? You are indirectly killing your father Abraham, because Abraham came to be David and David came to be Christ, the Anointed One the King. The King is one! Abraham was a king. David was a king and Jesus Christ, the KING of Kings. What this means is that you are all Kings and Queens and Princes and

Princesses. Consequently, every human being on earth is a child of THE FATHER GOD.

Therefore, in Christ who is The KING of Kings and the LORD of Lords the final Adam, the spiritual Adam? The whole human race is one. Accordingly, there is no tribalism again. No segregation and no more envy.

The fruit of peace is sown for the peacemakers. That means the children of God. **THE FATHER GOD** is now called **THE SUPREME PEACE**. And the children are called PEACEMAKERS. The grandchildren are now called mercy, love, honesty and the rest of the virtues of **THE FATHER GOD,** so tell **ME** whom you are going to kill. The energy is now growing in the salvation of humankind. Love one another and be in unity with all creation. It is one nation, one peace, one love, one spirit of equality and one currency. Everything is one. There is no negative to operate again.

Do NOT USE ANY EMBLEM OF ANIMALS including dragon, lion, bird, fish and all the rest of them for anything and on anything. If you do, **I** THE SUPREME WORD OF THE UNIVERSE shall destroy those ideas. USE HUMAN BEINGS, A MAN AND A WOMAN FOR YOUR EMBLEMS, WITH THE LIGHT OF THE FATHER GOD ON TOP OF IT. That light represents THE SUPREME WORD. That is the type of emblem **I** authorize. THE SUPREME WORD lives in the human beings.

Don't celebrate death, but celebrate life, because life is continuation. Death is to recycle. That is why **I** call Africa, the Conclusion of the Cycle.

Cycle is turning round and around. It is turning things around and joining them up again. That is, recycling something and it goes into use and returns for recycling and again it goes out, and so you repeat and repeat, again and again. So, it goes on non-stop. In the spirit, it is cycle of the physical and the soul but in the soul it is recycle. Recycle means rebirth. Cycle means the SPIRIT, the destination and the source and that is ZAKROLL OOO.

All this information is intact in this Lecture Revelation.

D: **ONE SPIRIT ONE LOVE ONE LIFE AND ONE FATHER AND MOTHER OF ALL THINGS BROTHERHOOD**

Everything is one from the SPIRIT ALL THINGS THE SPOKEN WORD. THE SPOKEN WORD manifested all creations through love, ONE Love. It is that ONE Love that lives in every human's nature as human beings life and in every living organism.

Human beings are only authorized to eat only living organisms to survive the physical life. ALL LIVING CREATURES MUST EAT ONLY LIVING ORGANISMS. DON'T EAT ANY LIVING SOUL that is, fishes, birds animals and man. All the four living creatures' viz., man, animals, birds and fish should ONLY eat living organisms, which are FRUITS and HERBS or VEGETABLES. Then you all LIVE AS ONE ENTITY OF LOVE. That is the Paradise of THE FATHER GOD established on earth from now on. You are all Brotherhood, one brethren from ONE parent called BROTHERHOOD of the CROSS and STAR.

CROSS and STAR means tolerance. The journey so far to arrive here has been a tedious and that is the CROSS. Then, the STAR is SUCCESS that we are in now. We are no more in the CROSS. In other words, if you answer to yourself Christian, Muslim, Judaist, Buddhist or whatsoever else you call yourself or even God and you still hate and practice evil, and practice any act of wickedness on somebody or you harm somebody in any manner at all seen or unseen, you are still in the CROSS. You have NOT PASSED that CROSS. In contrast, if you LOVE ONE ANOTHER you have passed the cross to STAR and you will live with THE FATHER GOD forever.

This SUPREME FUTURE of LOVE is for those who passed from Natural Brotherhood to the SPIRITUAL BROTHERHOOD OF THE STAR OF THE FATHER GOD. That means you carried the Cross of Christ of LOVE ONE ANOTHER then you succeeded to live together.

When Christians and Muslims live together without killing one another, when no one fight anymore for land, when America and Britain and Iraq and Iran and Afghanistan, live together without fighting and killing one another, then you are in the STAR! When Russia, Georgia, Ossetia and the rest of them stop fighting, hating and killing one another, when Liberia, Congo, Sierra Leone, Somali and other warring parties live together without killing one another, then you are in the STAR! When China, India Pakistan and the rest stop killing one another, then you are in the STAR! When all of Africa, all of

Asia, all of the America's, all of Europe and indeed the whole world lives peacefully together, then the whole world is in the STAR!

Remember this that, when you are still fighting and still having differences, you are in the CROSS and you will be crucified with that darkness spirit now if you don't change for good to be in the STAR with **THE FATHER GOD**.

E: **I MEAN BUSINESS NOW!**

What you are reading now is **MY PROPER BUSINESS OF I, THE FATHER GOD THE CREATOR OF THE UNIVERSE**, the **ONE** who created you, the **ONE** that talks through you, the **ONE** that lives in you. Don't deceive yourself that you are in the hands of any other power or anything you think that makes you to survive whether juju, secret society or the occultism you practice or you entered into anything that you think makes you to have power or to live life. **I, THE FATHER GOD**, controls those things. Whatsoever and wherever you think you keep yourself, it is via **THE SPOKEN WORD** and you exist through **MY** SPIRIT the ENERGY of **THE SUPREME BEING**. Therefore, do not allow yourself to be deceived in the evil thought. **I** MEAN BUSINESS NOW!

I MEAN BUSINESS therefore you will fill the impact of THE GREAT UNIVERSAL CHANGE!

The whole world should live in peace, but before that anyone who reject **MY WORD, I THE SUPREME WORD THE FATHER GOD** will decide what to do, and where to keep such individual human being who do not want to practice Love, oneness, unity, equality, mercy and peace with all men. I say from now:

No more fighting!
No quarrelling!
No war!
No segregation!
No tribalism!
No division!

Everywhere, here and there should be one **LOVE**.

If you are big and prominent and cover everywhere, try and be ONE with everyone. If you can do anything to be one with everybody, do it. Anything anybody can do to bring goodness, to bring joy, to bring happiness, to bring peace, to bring cooperation, to bring any positive thing to the whole world, try and do it. **MY** Holy Spirit of Truth will support you.

If on the contrary, you go to do any sort of wickedness anywhere, cause segregation, plan any sort of evil or teach people how to do bad things then you are going to be DESTROYED!

Even by hearing this information, **I** BARRIER ALL NEGATIVISMS, ALL HINDRANCES, ALL EVIL, and ALL ELEMENTARY BEHAVIOURS OF AKPAN. '**I** am the first, I am the second, I am this and I am that.' I have put up barriers against all those elementary behaviours. What you have now is to be one. YOU ARE ONE. LOVE ONE ANOTHER.

You are peacemakers all over the world.

Muslims are peacemakers.

Christians are peacemakers.

When you reason wrongly and say that if you kill you go to heaven, which heaven have you been up till now? You only come back to commit suicide and kill yourself again. For how long are you going to continue to come back on earth TO TIE BOMB YOURSELF AND BOMB YOURSELF and come back to bomb yourself again and repeat your actions again and again and again and also killing others along with you AND SAY YOU ARE GOING TO HEAVEN and that you are going to be a martyr? YOU ARE NOT GOING TO ANY HEAVEN! And you are not going to be martyr for anything. **I THE SUPREME WORD THE FATHER GOD ALMIGHTY, THE CREATOR OF THE UNIVERSE** that CREATED you says to you that you are NOT going to any Heaven for strapping bomb on yourself and killing yourself and others! And any country, individual or group of human beings go about killing people in any form, you will be sorry for your evil soul, what **I THE FATHER GOD THE CREATOR OF UNIVERSE** will do to you. You are dead and you are suffering! You are restless and riddled with problems all over you and all over your place! The only thing that you must do now since AKPAN'S Spirit has come back is to LOVE ONE ANOTHER is to STOP BOMBING ANYONE OR YOURSELF again!

AFRICA THE FIRST FATHER IS solid-skin or AKWA OWO and you are intelligent, peaceful, have humility and peace and joy.

You must rule the world with peace.

You must control the world with oneness.

You must have the security of people in your heart.

NOT the security to kill people.

NOT the security to go to war.

You must have security in love, kindness and humility. When you are humble, you acquire power. If you have loved that is the utmost power.

Use love, use humility, use kindness to rule the world and **I THE FATHER GOD** will be by you and in you to progress your nation, and call you **THE BLESSED NATION OF UNITY, LOVE AND PEACE**. Show yourself as the father if you are the positive father. Show yourself as the mother if you are the positive mother. THE SUPREME MOTHER OF KINDNESS, THE SUPREME MOTHER OF PEACE, THE SUPREME MOTHER OF BLESSING and THE FATHER GOD have all come down on earth. **I** THE FATHER GOD ALMIGHTY HAS COME WITH ALL HIS ENTOURAGE FROM HEAVEN AND PERFECT PEACE NOW REIGNS ON EARTH.

From today! I have solved all the problems of the entire world between Christians and Muslims, between Ishmael and Isaac, Abraham's children, between Esau and Jacob, between Adam and Eve including all the negative people. There is no negativism anymore.

Stop forming any club called secret society. There is nothing secret again. Just LOVE ONE ANOTHER. If you want power, you should love. All the power you want you can acquire by LOVING ONE ANOTHER because all the spirits will unite with you and you will become powerful. But if you hate you die. That is what hatred causes.

Don't drink any blood. There is no more blood for you to drink. All the spirits or souls that live through drinking blood are all going to melt away one by one and will all finish because there is no blood for them to drink anymore. If you drink any blood, you will die both spirit and soul. There is no evil that will survive anymore from today, now and forever more. Amen.

F: ENOUGH IS ENOUGH!

Enough Is Enough! **I** have had enough! You see the journey so far, which is from the time of creation of things unseen and things seen to the physical creation of The Spoken Word to Adam and Eve to the present world of today, is it not tedious? Supposed **I AM** not **LOVE**, what do you think would have happened? **I** created humankind in **MY** image and likeness and **I** live in every human being. Is it not stupidity to delude yourself with what you think you are and can do? Whom are you using to cause all these problems? Is it not **ME THE FATHER GOD THE SUPREME WORD**?

Without WORD, will you go to war?

Without WORD, will you have life to create nuclear weapons and all other war armaments?

Without WORD, will you have life to come to hate anybody? What will any human being do without WORD?

I AM THE WORD THAT IS TALKING. If you think you don't believe in **ME** then, you should drop that WORD! Don't speak again! If you speak, again this WORD is against you and your conscience.

If you come across this Lecture Revelation, make sure you give it to someone else.

EVERY HUMAN BEING SHOULD GIVE SEVEN **FATHER'S TALK (GOD PRESENT)** LECTURES REVELATIONS TO ANOTHER SEVEN PEOPLE.

Make sure that seven human beings read seven of THE **FATHER'S TALK (GOD PRESENT)** Lectures Revelations then you have finished your assignment with those souls. Pass them on in a positive way to others so that the INFORMATION of **THE FATHER GOD** contained in **THE FATHER'S TALK (GOD PRESENT)** will reach every human being on earth. THAT IS THE WORK **I** GIVE TO EVERY HUMAN BEING. Then, partake fully and happily in *THE UNIVERSAL SUPREME WORD SEASON*

CELEBRATION. All is well with humankind. That is **THE REMEDY**.

DON'T fight again!

DON'T struggle for anything!

DON'T go to settle problems with war to make peace!

Make peace internally in you.

Make peace with understanding and wisdom.

Let the higherself make peace with elementary self to understand one another. LOVE ONE ANOTHER to have all the problems solved. **I HAVE HAD ENOUGH! ENOUGH IS ENOUGH!**

DON'T go to trigger any problem in any country saying that you are rendering help. Don't help anybody in that manner. Help yourself first. Check your mind first that YOU LOVE ONE ANOTHER then, you would know exactly what to do in other to HELP ONE ANOTHER.

G: ESIEN EMANA AKPAN ENDED WITH THE FATHER GOD ALMIGHTY

I THE SUPREME WORD OF THE UNIVERSE, who created AKPAN and preserved AKPAN, have come to solve that problem of **AKPAN** through this advice. In the beginning was the **WORD** and the **WORD** was with **GOD** of **AKPAN** and the **WORD** was **GOD** in the human form. So, that **WORD** is NOW TALKING.

Forgive One Another.
Believe that everything is well.
Muslims, don't kill Christians. Christians don't kill Muslims because you are killing yourself by doing that. When you kill and come back to kill and to kill again and again and finally kill your-self by committing suicide. But, if you decide that from today, you are not going to hate or kill again, your soul has taken evolution to be among the peacemaking groups of human beings, and then all is well with you. Even if you died and came

back, you will live well because **I** have removed your soul from the basket of committing suicide to that of life.

Judas Iscariot was the copy of Cain. What did he do? He committed suicide. Another incarnate of Cain was Absalom. **I** stopped AKPAN (first son) not to rule because of this problem of **ESIEN EMANA AKPAN**. If all AKPAN partake fully in THE UNIVERSAL SUPREME WORD SEASON CELEBRATION and LOVE ONE ANOTHER then every first position and everything first will start being good things from now on, and Satan will not use you again. Try and see.

All women will remain married as the first wives. No man will leave you for a second wife. The problem of AKPAN is responsible for the marriages that break into pieces. That was what affected Sarah. She had no peace married to Abraham. Then she had to ask her house girl to go away. And when Hagar left with Ishmael the physical first son of Abraham the whole trouble was on top of her head.

Was she happy then? Of course not! She was not happy! She struggled for first position.

If you struggle for FIRST, you will have problems. Look at Muslims who are Ishmael nation, fighting, quarrelling and killing everybody because they were refused the First Position. The first son, is it a good thing? Do you think FIRST is a very good thing? Is it not the FIRST problem that stretched till today?

If you knew the problems that followed the first, you will be so happy to be udoh (second son). Don't even be the last as well. Therefore, do not fight for what you do not know. Humility is the key of life. Don't struggle to be in the first position and don't allow yourself to be in the last position. Struggle to be in the middle and love. Therefore, that is the special advice today.

ESIEN EMANA AKPAN, problem of the first position, which is the problem of ignorance, the problem of elementary self, has ended through

The Holy Spirit of Truth and your eyes are now opened. The SPIRIT of **THE FATHER GOD** has opened the eyes of humankind. And all is well with humankind AMEN.

H: **NO MORE NEGATIVE SELF GLORY**

Do not give glory to death.
Do not give glory to Satan.
Do not give glory to evil.
Do not give glory to juju.
Do not give glory to animals, birds or fishes.
LET ALL GLORY GO TO THE SUPREME WORD OF THE UNIVERSE, THE ONE WHO CREATED YOU THE FATHER GOD, THE SPIRIT.
HONOUR THE SPIRIT. Fear **GOD**.
Honour the KING of Kings and the LORD of Lords, THE SUPREME WORD.
LOVE ONE ANOTHER.
LOVE is as money, it needs to be in every individual purse, so Love needs to live in every heart. If you love well

and do not plan evil against somebody then you are not even able to raise your hands to beat somebody much more killing the person. You are a correct person a copy of the human God.

Cain has no representative, but Abel has. Therefore, from today all of you came out from the tribe of Abel. He is life preserver. And the spirit of Cain is now ended and changed for good, IN THE NAME AND BLOOD OF OUR LORD JESUS CHRIST. Amen.

I: **ONLY THE POSITIVE OF MYSELF SHALL BE GLORIFIED FROM NOW**

FROM NOW AND FOR ETERNITY ONLY THE POSITIVE SIDE OF THE FATHER GOD SHALL BE GLORIFIED. When you think well, speak well, hear well, see well and do well that is the **GLORY OF THE FATHER GOD**.

When you do good things, good follow you. The good things you do will posterized your name.

No more glory for the negative.

No more glory for going to war. **I** have condemned that. If you honour anyone for going to war, **I** will dishonour you and also condemn you.

Do not think that someone will come and sit in the court to judge you. Your conscience will now start to judge you. The conscience of everybody on earth will start to judge him or her right from this moment.

This year **TWO THOUSAND AND EIGHT IS THE GLORIOUS YEAR OF THE FATHER GOD**, and the beginning of the **GLORIOUS YEARS OF THE FATHER GOD**. I have launched the new universe and it will materialize whenever it pleases **ME** from spirit to the physical because it is from spirit to soul and from soul to the physical reality. That is to say, that **THE SUPREME FUTURE** has already spiritually been set and it will come to pass.

If you practice wickedness and evil, you will not be born to be amongst those to be in **THE SUPREME FUTURE**. You will be in wastebasket.

But if you practice good things, **I** will promote your soul and give you a spiritual certificate. You will then take evolution to **THE SUPREME FUTURE** where you will enjoy and be happy.

This world **I** mean it! Everybody shall live without fear. You will travel to anywhere and not be afraid of anything. Only natural things will happen. Nobody will cause anything to happen to anybody or at anywhere. There will be NO sound of guns and bombs.

There will be NO sound of shooting and bombing.

There will be NO sound of hatred.

The only sounds that will be heard are that of singing. You will only hear singing of songs happily, rejoicing with one another and sharing with one another. There will be peace and unity and love and oneness all over the world. There will be no difference between dark-skin human beings and light-skin human beings. There will be no difference between one colour of skin and another colour of skin.

Everybody will be, ONE equals to **GOD PRESENT**.

AO: **THERE IS PEACE EVERYWHERE HERE AND THERE IN THE ENTIRE UNIVERSE**

THERE WILL BE PEACE EVERYWHERE, HERE AND THERE IN THE ENTIRE UNIVERSE. Everybody will celebrate THE SUPREME WORD by participating in **THE UNIVERSAL SUPREME WORD SEASON CELEBRATION**, a yearly celebration for eternity. Join the group of peacemakers.

I have ordered HIS ROYAL MAJESTY KING SOLOMON DAVID JESSE ETE the Senior Christ Servant, the incarnate Abel to establish **THE UNIVERSAL PEACEMAKERS ORGANIZATION** along with **THE UNIVERSAL SUPREME WORD SEASON CELEBRATION** on earth.

If you like to, you can connect to be in that organization.
PEACEMAKERS ARE THE

CHILDREN OF THE FATHER GOD. Those are the people **I** will engineer their soul to inherit the world. Therefore, all killing implements must be dropped.

All KNIVES should be drooped!
All GUNS should be dropped!
All ARROWS should be dropped!

Anything that means pointing fingers at someone or thinking evil against someone or doing evil to someone should be dropped from today. Make PEACE!

Peace means Solomon. Peace is on earth. Love amongst humankind shall continue to reign supreme in the entire world.

Don't dwell on colour of any human being. Dark-skin human being can rule. Light-skin human being can rule. Any human being of any other colour can rule provided you have love. Do not struggle for any position. Wherever nature keeps, you take it, be there and do good things, witness the good work for **GOD**. You are all

Servants of **THE FATHER GOD ALMIGHTY**.

I am the first son. No more!
I am the second son. No more!
I am the king. No more!
I am a queen. No more!
I am the president. No more!
I am the prime minister. No more!

Everybody is a servant of God. Nevertheless those names and titles exist for administrative purposes.

LET MY PEACE AND BLESSING ABIDE WITH THE ENTIRE WORLD, WITH ENTIRE MUSLIMS, WITH ENTIRE CHRISTIANS, WITH ENTIRE JUDAIST, WITH ENTIRE AKPAN, WITH ENTIRE FIRST POSITIONS "AFRICA", NOW AND FOREVER MORE. AMEN!

THANK YOU FATHER!

Chapter Five
THE INSPIRATIONAL WRITER

KING SOLOMON SPIRITUAL LIBRARY
THE GOD ENCYCLOPAEDIA WORD OF INFINITY

INSPIRATIONAL WRITERS AND READERS OF THE
FATHER'S TALK
(GOD PRESENT)
KING SOLOMON SPIRITUAL LIBRARY

In the name of our Lord Jesus Christ, In the blood of our Lord Jesus Christ, Now and forever more, Amien

(A) REFERENCING THE FATHER'S TALK (GOD PRESENT) IN KING SOLOMON SPIRITUAL LIBRARY

I know that some people will be inspired when they visit King Solomon Spiritual Library website or bookshop, and have access to any of **THE FATHER'S TALK (GOD PRESENT)** information through books, electronics, audio and otherwise and are inspired to write or produce any information through the knowledge that they have gained, they must not fail to reference **THE FATHER'S TALK (GOD PRESENT)** in **King**

Solomon Spiritual Library as the source of your inspirations.

(B) THE WORD OF TRUTH AND THE HOLY SPIRIT PRINCIPLES

Since **THE FATHER'S TALK** (**GOD PRESENT**) is the direct information from **I THE FATHER GOD ALMIGHTY HIMSELF**, all positive children of **GOD** can be, and will be inspired with this **WORD** because the **WORD** of **THE FATHER GOD, THE CREATOR OF THE UNIVERSE** is a Spiritual Case Study for all souls to improve to have self awareness and a Higherself Consciousness.

When you are inspired and you want to write, make sure that your ideas, principles and concepts are based on the Holy Spirit of Truth without changing the ordinance of the **FATHER'S TALK (GOD PRESENT)**.

(C) THERE SHALL BE CONSEQUENCES THAT WOULD FOLLOW THOSE WHO USE THE MEANING, THE CONCEPTS AND THE PRINCIPLES OF THE FATHER'S TALK (GOD PRESENT) FOR THE PURPOSES OF MISLEADING

Consequences shall follow those who use the meaning, the concepts and the principles of **THE FATHER'S TALK (GOD**

PRESENT) for the purposes of misleading in any manner.

Any Human-God, human-animal, human-bird or human-fish who has access to **THE FATHER'S TALK** (**GOD PRESENT**) through any means, be it via books, electronics, audio and otherwise should know that those words are not the words of human beings. The words are transcribed, proofread and accepted by **ME THE FATHER GOD** as it comes from the **SUPREME STUDIO OF THE ALMIGHTY FATHER GOD HIMSELF**, via **King Solomon Spiritual Library**.

When the signal of the information alerts HRM King Solomon David Jesse **ETE** from **I THE FATHER** through the **COMPREHENSIVE MEMORY OF GOD** in Him, at anytime in the day or at night and anywhere, whether on the road or any public place, he will take note of the title of the Revelation Lectures. Sometimes if the location is conducive, lectures can take place immediately. If the location is not conducive, **I THE FATHER GOD** fixes the time for the full Lecture Revelation to take place. Most of the time, some of the Lecture Revelations take about a week, a month or six months and so on, to deliver when **I THE FATHER GOD** brings it back from **HIS SUPREME MEMORY** to HRM King Solomon **ETE**.

Take note that the information of **THE FATHER'S TALK (GOD PRESENT)** is not preaching, or the giving of sermons or shared discussion. **THE FATHER GOD** calls them "***LECTURE***

REVELATIONS", which is a Spiritual Case Study for humankind to improve and have the Higherself Consciousness about himself or herself and their **CREATOR**.

For this reason, every human being that comes across any of the information of the **FATHER'S TALK (GOD PRESENT)** should treat it with utmost and absolute respect and reverence at all times.

HRM King Solomon David Jesse **ETE** is not responsible for **THE FATHER'S TALK (GOD PRESENT)** but **ME, THE FATHER GOD HIMSELF. I, THE ALMIGHTY FATHER** only use Him as a way through, just like a loud speaker from the radio or television receiver.

For this reason, HRM King Solomon David Jesse **ETE** will not be held responsible by anyone who does not understand the contents, the concepts and the principles of **THE FATHER'S TALK (GOD PRESENT)** information in King Solomon Spiritual Library. He will not answer any questions or queries from spirit to soul and the physical truth in connection to the above from the lower mind individuals, persons or groups. However, if you are positive and you have love and are humble, have patience and are peaceful and you want to know and understand more of any part of **THE FATHER'S TALK (GOD PRESENT)**; '**You should use fasting and prayer**' and or if anyone has any questions in good faith, he or she is free to write to HRM King Solomon and **THE FATHER** in him will respond. He will not, and there is no response to any questions, queries and anything negative with the craftiness of the evil minds of humankind.

That is why you should first read seven **FATHER'S TALK (GOD PRESENT)** Lecture Revelations before commenting and

THE FATHER GOD with **HIS SUPREME HOLY SPIRIT OF TRUTH** will bless all those who read and accept this information with good faith through the name and blood of our Lord Jesus Christ, *Amien*.

In the name of our Lord Jesus Christ In the blood of our Lord Jesus Christ Now and forever more, Amen

ESTABLISH MY SPIRITUAL LIBRARY

I THE FATHER GOD ALMIGHTY THE SUPREME WORD OF THE UNIVERSE AM THE SPIRITUAL FOOD TO FEED YOUR SOUL. Therefore, **I** want every family in this world, every home in this world, every office, government offices, monarchies, countries, states, regions, counties, communities, local authority compounds, family homes and everyone and everywhere to collect published copies of **THE EVERLASTING GOSPEL AND THE FATHER'S TALK (GOD PRESENT)** Lecture

Revelations of **KING SOLOMON SPIRITUAL LIBRARY** and establish it physically in your houses. This is so that everybody would have these RECORDS. Go to read the books regularly. Every family should have a Library of **MY INFORMATION CENTRE** for their family members.

Every generation of a particular family should be able to easily go to their family Library of KING SOLOMON SPIRITUAL LIBRARY EVERLASTING GOSPEL and the **FATHER'S TALK (GOD PRESENT) Lecture Revelations** and read the Gospels and Lecture Revelations so that generations upon generations will access their KING SOLOMON SPIRITUAL LIBRARY.

You must all have **THE LIBRARY OF THE FATHER GOD ALMIGHTY** called **KING**

SOLOMON SPIRITUAL LIBRARY THE FATHER'S TALK (GOD PRESENT) LECTURE REVELATIONS in your homes and offices. The authorities and individuals concerned must see to that. When you establish your branch of KING SOLOMON SPIRITUAL LIBRARY and have the **EVERLASTING GOSPELS** and the **FATHER'S TALK (GOD PRESENT)** Lecture Revelations then that place is blessed and secured. In the name and Blood of Our Lord Jesus Christ, now and forever more, *Amien*.

THANK YOU FATHER

> **"THEUNISAL-SUREME SEACELION"**
> The Universal Supreme Season Celebration
> =========
> **"THEUNI-SUREME WORA THECRO-THEUNISE"**
> **The Universal Supreme Word Almighty**
> **The Creator Of The Universe**
> ==================
> **WWW.COME4WORD.COM**

THE OFFICIAL SITE FOR
==============
EVERLASTING UNIVERSAL ALL WORD SEASON APPRECIATION

CEREMONIAL PROGRAM
=======

===

THE UNIVERSAL SUPREME ALL WORD

SEASON CELEBRATION (GOD PRESENT) SOMETHING MORE THAN 'GOLD' THE HEART OF ALL MEN IS WORD

===================
THE WORD IS THE MAKER, THE SOLE ADMINISTRATOR AND THE CREATOR OF THE UNIVERSE THEREFORE, ALL HUMANKIND ON EARTH MUST APPRECIATE THE WORD IN ALL CAPACITIES FOREVER
===============
FROM EVERY OA OF AO TO AO OF AO (1st OCTOBER TO 10th OCTOBER). YEARLY IS THE UNIVERSAL SUPREME

ALL WORD SEASON
CELEBRATION TO APPRECIATE THE FATHER GOD ALMIGHTY
=================
CELEBRATION! CELEBRATION!! CELEBRATION!!!
THE UNIVERSAL

SUPREME WORD CELEBRATION OF ALL TIME

=======

THE

ALMIGHTY FATHER GOD, THE CREATOR OF ALL THINGS BROTHERHOOD

**ORGANISED BY
KING SOLOMON
SPIRITUAL LIBRARY
=======
HRM KING SOLOMON
DAVID JESSE ETE
INSPIRATIONAL HEAD**

**IN THE HONOUR OF THE
FATHER GOD THE
CREATOR OF
THE UNIVERSE
THE HOLY SPIRIT OF
TRUTH
AND THE KING OF KINGS
AND THE LORD OF LORDS
==========
THANK YOU FATHER**

KING SOLOMON SPIRITUAL LIBRARY

THE GOD ENCYCLOPAEDIA WORD OF INFINITY

=============

King Solomon Spiritual Library, God Universal Information Centre
FATHER'S TALK (GOD PRESENT)

WITH LOVE

Covered: **This BOOK,** e-book, software or software's, books, websites, videos, audios, idea or ideas, formula or formulas, manual or instruction manual

... Hereby gives you a non-exclusive license to use the ... (THIS BOOK).

Some of the words here are coded with the (WORD OF SUPER HOLY AND INTELLIGENCE FATHER GOD ALMIGHTY)

Title, ownership rights, and intellectual property rights in and to the Website, Books, E-book, Audios and Videos, Shops and Store – e-Stores, Fundraisings, Celebrations and the Supreme Word Seasons Celebration formulas and arrangements, Positive Inspiration, HOLY (FATA),

FATHER GOD ALMIGHTY POSSESSING SPIRIT in thought, in words and in deed, thinking well, speaking well, hearing well and doing well shall remain in me and in ... The BOOK is protected by international copyright.

FATHER'S TALK (GOD PRESENT)

The message in **THE FATHER'S TALK (GOD PRESENT)** does not challenge any authority as individuals, groups or governments of any land or even any belief of any form. It is rather challenging the truth that is hidden from mankind. Therefore, any spirit, soul or physical human being who decides to challenge this truth shall have himself or herself to blame.

Key A: Any individual that reads any of **THE FATHER'S TALK** (GOD PRESENT) with faith; love and acceptance will experience immediate positive change in his or her life from spirit, soul to physical. If he or she accepts the message then he or she will be free from any evil.

Key B: **PEACE AND LOVE**
If you do not believe the contents of any of **THE FATHER'S TALK (GOD PRESENT),** it is possible through **THE FATHER'S** divine love and peace to simply hand over your copy to a friend or somebody else that would like to keep a copy, or by signing out from any of the websites that connect to **THE FATHER'S TALK (GOD**

PRESENT) and KING SOLOMON SPIRITUAL e-LIBRARY without any evil and negative comments then you are blessed and free.

========

FROM THE DESK OF THE INSPIRATIONAL HEAD

Fees, Prices and Donations; There is no refund on fees, prices or donations since your fees, priced payments or donations are used as a charity contribution to do administrative work of **THE SUPREME WORD**, so please kindly read this first before you decide to involve yourself in any of the under mentioned of HRM King Solomon David Jesse **ETE** universal Inspirational Businesses of (**GOD PRESENT**) in cash, kind and otherwise.

I CAME FROM THE FATHER GOD, WITH THE FATHER GOD,

AND BY THE FATHER GOD TO ESTABLISH THE FOLLOWING: THE FATHER'S TALK (GOD PRESENT), The Spiritual Advice, Healing and Counselling on General Live (The Universal Supreme Spiritual General Hospital), New Songs and Psalms of King David and Solomon, The Word of **GOD** Processing City in Ikot Okwo or e-City online, The Trinity Celebration, **"OUC FUND"**, The Universal Bank Account For All Creations, **"ERUFA"** ETE Royal Universal Family, **"THEUNISAL-SUREME SEACELION"** The Universal Supreme Word Season Celebration To Appreciate **THE FATHER GOD ALMIGHTY "THEUNI-SUREME WORA THECRO-THEUNISE"** The Universal Supreme Word Almighty, THE CREATOR OF THE UNIVERSE. Therefore all distributors and contributors should attach and make this information available to all readers, website visitors, distributors, affiliates person/group, celebrant and celebrations centres, supporters and promoters, members, workers and voluntary workers, Ete royal universal palace committee, governments and many other centres as an agreement. Please kindly know that I am not answering to any physical human except **PEACE, UNITY AND LOVE.**

"**THEUNISAL-SUREME WORA THECRO-THEUNISE**".

I AM IN THE STAGE OF SUPER HOLY AND INTELLIGENT FATHER GOD POSITIVE MADNESS OF THE HOLY SPIRIT OF TRUTH,

ENYEN ODUDU ODUDU ODUDU ABASI MI OOO ZIM ZIM ZIM ASSASU, POSITIVE POSITIVE POSITIVE. UKEMEKE AKA IDIOK UNAM.

Let the peace and blessing of THE HOLY FATHER abide with everyone who corporates with this divine **FATHER'S TALK (GOD PRESENT)**

THANK YOU FATHER
BY
THE HOLY SPIRIT OF
THE FATHER GOD
THROUGH HIS SERVANT
The Senior Christ Servant
HRM King Solomon David Jesse **ETE**
Brotherhood of the
Cross and STAR
Eteroyal Universal family
Ikot Okwo The Great City of Refuge,
Ete Community
Ikot Abasi LGA-543001
Akwa Ibom State Nigeria-W/A
Tel. 08036693841

Website: www.ksslibrary.com
Email: ksslibrary@eteroyalmail.com

==============

READ AT LEAST SEVEN LECTURE REVELATIONS BEFORE YOU CAN MAKE ANY COMMENTS

In the Name of Our Lord Jesus Christ, In the Blood of Our Lord Jesus Christ, Now and forever more

Everybody should have access to and read at least seven **FATHER'S TALK** (**GOD PRESENT**) Lecture Revelations before making any comments about it. If you do not go through at least seven **FATHER'S TALK** Lecture Revelations and you comment, you may make mistakes. And when you make mistakes your blood will be upon you because you would have taken voluntary evolution to misquote **THE FATHER GOD THE CREATOR OF THE UNIVERSE**.

One of **THE FATHER'S TALK** stands for one SPIRIT of GOD, which means that THE **FATHER'S TALK** (**GOD PRESENT**) Lecture Revelations are witnessed by the Seven SPIRITS of GOD, which **I** use as the Seven Churches of GOD and Seven days of the Week, Seven spirits of Creation in one Supreme energy of **THE FATHER GOD**,

THE SPOKEN WORD therefore,

when you read seven **FATHER'S TALK** (**GOD PRESENT**) Lecture Revelations then, **I, THE FATHER GOD** will reveal you as a positive person and then you will have a portion in **ME**. And one of **THE FATHER'S TALK** (**GOD PRESENT**) will have a portion in you. Then you would know that this information came from **THE FATHER GOD**. **THE FATHER'S TALK** (**GOD PRESENT**) is not a mere talk from a man!

In the Name of Our Lord Jesus Christ, In the Blood of Our Lord Jesus Christ, Now and forever more

INVITATION
====
THE UNIVERSAL SUPREME ACKNOWLEDGEMENT

'THE ONLY SOURCE
AND REMEDY
TO END ALL HUMANITY
PROBLEMS'
Join me to Celebrate;
Acknowledge,

Appreciate and give full
RECOGNITION to
THE UNIVERSAL
SUPREME WORD,
YOUR LIFE FORCE,
THE TOTALITY OF ALL
TOTALITIES
YOUR CREATOR,
THE FATHER GOD
ALMIGHTY,
THE CREATOR OF THE
UNIVERSE

WWW.KSSLIBRARY.COM
WWW.COME4WORD.COM
WWW.THEWORDCITY.COM
WWW.KINGSOLOMONSPIRITUALLIBRARY.COM

Contact EMAIL:
hrmkingsolomon@eteroyalmail.com

THANK YOU FATHER

The title List of some of the

FATHER'S TALK
(GOD PRESENT)

1: THE MANUAL OF THE SPOKEN WORD

2: THE MANUAL OF LIFE

3: INVESTMENT WITH GOD

4: ISO IBOT EDEM IBOT

5: THE CHARACTER OF THE NEW WORLD

6: HELPMANTRANS

7: UNDERSTANDING MY WORD

8: TRUTH, POSITION, POST AND NAME

9: NON STOP BLESSING

10: IMPRESSION

11: STAGES OF EDUCATIONS (SPE, SSE & SUE)

12: THE ENGINEERING OF LIFE

13: THE CONTENT PACKAGE

14: THE BUDGET OF THE NEW WORLD

15: DIVINE ATTENTION

16: THE BABY SPIRIT

17: PROMOTION

18: ADVANCE AND PROGRESSING MIND

19: THE TEMPLE OF THE LIVING GOD

20: I AM OK

21: THE SPIRIT OF TRUTH

22: THE PERFECT PERMANENCY

23: THE FATHER GOD, GOD, GOD THE FATHER

24: HUSBAND, WIFE AND CHILD

25: GOD AND HIS HARBINGER

26: LIFE EVERLASTING

27: POSSESS

28: MY MIND AND MY PLAN

29: AFTER HEART AND AFTER MIND

30: MY DECLARATION & STAND IN BCS

31: BEYOND THE HOPE OF FAITH

32: MENTAL STAIN

33: THE PRINCIPLE OF SELF HOLD

34: THE MASTERSHIP

35: HIDU-CUM

36: THE UNIVERSAL PARENT

37: ADVANCED YOU AND ME

38: THE GREAT UNIVERSAL CHANGE

39: THE PROJECTED MIND

40: INDESTRUCTIBLE BLESSED FIVE STARS

41: ASTROTS, GOD PRESENT I AND MY FATHER

42: SONGS THE COMPLETION

43: THE RIGHT BUTTON

44: AKWA ABASI IBOM- ETE - DIRECTING NDITO AKWA IBOM

45: THE DIGITAL AGE

46: GOD IS OFFICIAL CHAMPION

47: A TRUE WITNESS

48: MYSTERY OF PROCREATION AND BIRTH

49: THE UNIVERSAL UMBRELLA

50: THE FORERUNNER

51: A OF A TO Z (FIRST OF ALL)

52: MAN IN THREE CAPACITIES

53: THE TRUE LIFE OF HOLY SPIRIT PERSONIFIED

54: IN-BETWEEN THE FATHER & THE SON

55: DIVINE ARRANGEMENT & AUTHORITY

56: TWENTY FIRST CENTURY IS NOT FOR SATAN

57: THE SUPREME WORD SEASON CELEBRATION

58: THE MAXIMUM DEITY

59: TRANSFORMER TRANSMITTER AND WAVE

60: THE SUPREME FUTURE

61: THE BYLOVE OF WORD

62: THE SIGNATURE OF THE FATHER GOD

63: THE TWO WAYS

64: THE UNDERSTANDING OF LIFE

65: THE GREATER THAN SOLOMON IS HERE

66: THE CONQUEROR

67: THE SPIRITUAL GENERAL INSPECTOR OF LIFE

68: THE NIGERIA IN THE AFRICA Part one

69: THE NIGERIA IN THE AFRICA Part two

70: THE CREATOR AND CREATIONS PART ONE

71: THE CREATOR AND CREATIONS PART TWO

72: THE CREATOR AND CREATIONS PART THREE

73: THE SUPREME TEACHER

74: THE SPIRITUAL COVER

75: THE NIGERIA IN THE AFRICA PART THREE

76: THE SUPREME BELIEVE

77: CAST AND BAN (LECTURE IN LIVERPOOL)

78: LIFE EXTENSION MANUAL

79: THE SPIRITUAL TRAFFIC

80: THE VOICE OF THE CREATOR

81: MY OFFICE

82: LIFE SPIRITUAL FIRE EXTINGUISHER

83: INFORMATION

84: FATHER GOD FINAL ARRANGEMENT

85: THE LOVERS OF CHRIST

86: I LOVE YOU, I LOVE YOU TOO

87: THE UNIVERSAL SUPREME UPDATE

88: THE SUPREME ALTAR

89: THE SOURCE AND DESTINATION

90: A SON LIKE THE FATHER THE KING OF KINGS A ROOTS FROM HEAVEN (NOT THIS TIME AROUND)

91: THE TRUE WITNESS AND THE TRUE SERVANT

92: THE FINAL ARRANGEMENT

93: A TRUE NIGERIAN MAN AND WOMAN

94: EVERYONE MUST PERSONALLY INVOLVE

95: BEWARE

96: <u>ESIEN EMANA AKPAN "THE AFRICAN PROBLEMS"</u>

97: THE SECRET OF THE UNIVERSAL PROBLEMS AND THE REMEDY

(MUSLIM AND CHRISTIAN FROM THE SAME PARENT)

98: MMU-UDIM – THE BLESSED MOTHER (ABASI ME UDIM)

99: THINK WELL, SPEAK WELL AND DO WELL

100: THE STAGES OF HOW TO PROCESS THE WORD

101: EVIL STAIN, WHO RUNS AWAY FROM WHO

102: **BEYOND HUMAN KNOW PURELY SPIRITUAL**

103: **THE INSPIRATIONAL WRITER**

104: BIAKPAN OBIO AKPAN ABASI (THE NEW JERUSALEM CITY)

105: "OBAMA" THE STRAINTHEN AND THE SPIRIT OF BILL GATES AND MICROSOFT

106: THE HOLY TRINITY

107: AMEN –ODUWEM IKO ABASI

108: EVERYTHING – ALLTHINGS POSITIVE

109: OBLIGATIONS FOR ALL HUMAN BEINGS

THANK YOU FATHER

www.ingramcontent.com/pod-product-compliance
Lightning Source LLC
Chambersburg PA
CBHW021350290426
44108CB00010B/186